NOT JUST VERY FAST. BUT VERY GOOD.

There's a catch to using this book.

The Clean Team has timed and tested every sequence, technique, and product. They know what works. They tell you what to do. And they are The Boss.

They teach you a simple system for the whole house. They give you diagrams that help. They lead you step-by-step. They threaten you if you do it wrong!

The result is a sparkling clean home in under half the time you used to take. Very clean. Very fast. Very easy.

What's the catch? You do it their way. No arguments. No discussions. No compromises.

Why? Because it works!

SPEED CLEANING
FOR THOSE WHO WOULD RATHER BE DOING PRACTICALLY ANYTHING ELSE

"MAYBE YOU THINK YOU KNOW HOW TO CLEAN: IF SO, YOU CAN [STILL] PICK UP A FEW TIPS AND LEARN HOW TO WORK A LOT FASTER."

—*The Village Voice*

"THE MOST WORTHWHILE BOOK I'VE READ SINCE *THE JOY OF SEX*."

—L.G., Pepper Pike, Ohio

"Week 1 took me just over two hours. Week 2 took about an hour and 15 minutes. Week 3 took 56 minutes. Week 4 took 46 minutes. I'm sold."

—Michele Fagin, Vermont

"YOU MAY HAVE SAVED MY LIFE!"

—K.B.E., Minneapolis, Minn.

"I'm an industrial engineer and I have always felt my cleaning technique was efficient until I read yours. It really is amazing."

—B.M., Fairless Hills, Penn.

"*SPEED CLEANING* TELLS TRADE SECRETS THAT . . . WILL HELP ANYONE WORK FASTER AND MORE EFFICIENTLY."

—*Richmond Times-Dispatch*

"MY HUSBAND CAN'T BELIEVE I AM SO EXCITED ABOUT CLEANING HOUSE."
—S.B., Fort Worth, Texas

"CAMPBELL OFFERS MUCH EDUCATION IN THIS BOOK."
—*Rocky Mountain News*

"The first believable housecleaning book I have ever seen."
—M.V.B., Loma Linda, Calif.

"I THOUGHT IT WAS TERRIFIC! MY HUSBAND AND I BOTH WORK FULL TIME—I STAND BEHIND THE CLEAN TEAM SYSTEM 100 PERCENT."
—S. Brown, Illinois

"I LOVE YOUR BOOK!!! I HAVEN'T BEEN THIS EXCITED IN YEARS AND CERTAINLY *NEVER* ABOUT CLEANING. . . . I LOOK FORWARD TO CLEANING YOUR WAY. THANKS!"
—L. Sorg., Alexandria, Va.

"I HAVE NEVER READ SUCH AN ENLIGHTENING BOOK ON A SUBJECT THAT HAS MYSTIFIED MILLIONS OF WOMEN [AND MEN] SINCE THE BEGINNING OF TIME. BLESS YOU."
—B. McG., Madison, Wis.

Books by Jeff Campbell and The Clean Team

SPRING CLEANING
SPEED CLEANING
CLUTTER CONTROL
TALKING DIRT

SPEED CLEANING

Third Edition

Jeff Campbell
and
The Clean Team

A DELL TRADE PAPERBACK

Published by
Dell Publishing
a division of
Bantam Doubleday Dell Publishing Group, Inc.
1540 Broadway
New York, New York 10036

ISBN: 0-440-50374-4

Printed in the United States of America

June 1991

20 19 18

Acknowledgments

Bill Redican, editor and friend, contributed much of what is good, clever, and fun in this effort. He helped write and rewrite this whole project. Thank you.

Sarah Lazin, our agent, is one of those bright, successful, busy professional New York women that everyone reads about. She's always understood that our method of cleaning was meant to include professionals like her, and she's very good at explaining that to the right people.

Dedication

To my friends and partners at The Clean Team. Before them I mistakenly thought that work wasn't any fun. Thanks to them I look forward to weekdays also.

Table of Contents

INTRODUCTION TO THE THIRD EDITION

SPEED CLEANING was first published in 1987. More than ten years later, and just like the well-known batteries, it's still going strong.

I've been told that a book's average shelf life is only three weeks or so. That means *SPEED CLEANING* has endured approximately 173 times longer than average. Why? I believe it's because it makes such good sense in today's busy world. It will teach you how to do housecleaning in the very best way possible and in the most efficient way possible. And not by working harder. Just smarter! The result? You will reclaim that spare time that has vanished from your life.

A CLEAN GENE?

SPEED CLEANING was and is the first comprehensive solution to the housecleaning chores that each of us copes with and must find time for virtually every week of our lives. *SPEED CLEANING* finally paid attention to the fact that almost no one in our culture is actually taught *how* to do this. We seem to assume that if you drop someone in the middle of a dirty house, she (or he) would instinctively know how to go about getting it clean: sort of a cleaning gene at work. However, for those of us who arrived without the magic gene, *SPEED CLEANING* provides the very first step-by-step set of instructions on housecleaning. It's a proven method that furnishes even the most profoundly cleaning impaired the wherewithal to clean in the smartest way possible.

TIME

SPEED CLEANING also takes very, very seriously the amount of time that housecleaning consumes *and* the limited amount of time in which we have to do it. It's about time someone respected all those hours you spend scrubbing, dusting, and vacuuming. Whatever housecleaning skills most of us have were handed down by our mothers or grandmothers, who were able to do the work on a full-time basis. Given how our society has changed—now that so many women in America are working, commuting, *and* keeping house—those full-time cleaning methods no longer work. Full-time techniques won't fit into a weekend. Besides, not many of us look forward to spending precious weekends cleaning house. It's like going from one job to another.

LIKING IT?

SPEED CLEANING teaches new skills. Learning how to clean (or do anything else) the very best possible way can change how you feel about the activity. As you get better and better at a task, you move closer to the cutting edge of your attention. (Just watch a kid play a computer game.) As you get closer to that edge, it's nearly impossible to dislike what you're doing. When you learn how to shave off unnecessary steps, motions, and repetitions, you'll move closer and closer to full attention. You'll become a pure cleaning machine—a Ninja warrior of cleaning, if you wish.

If you already enjoy cleaning, the payoff is that you'll have a thoroughly clean house in as short a period of time as possible. It you *don't* enjoy cleaning, that's still not a problem. You'll get the same clean house, the same extra time for other activities, and you'll dislike it less.

POSITIVE FEEDBACK

I used to work for the telephone company. My work efforts were forwarded to various departments in paper form, and several weeks or months later a phone system would be installed—an event I might not even know about unless something went wrong. At its very best, I had precious little feedback for my efforts. By contrast, housecleaning offers a much more direct payoff. First the house was dirty and now it's clean, and whoever did it gets all the credit. Most of us don't stop to gloat over every item that gets cleaned, but each new bit of cleanliness provides a dose of straightforward positive feedback—the kind that's becoming increasingly rare.

EASE

Becoming an expert at what you do makes the activity itself easier. It's much easier to use a computer the 100th time or to change the oil in the lawn tractor the second or third time. When it comes to cleaning, it also turns out to be easier to work clockwise around a room once, cleaning from top to bottom and from back to front as you go, than it is to make fitful stops and starts and countless trips back and forth and up and down.

MORALE

Being an expert is also a morale booster. It's downright depressing to have a dirty house and not have the time to clean it. An almost universal lament in America has become: "I love a clean house, but I just don't have the time." In this situation, you either (a) give up and get depressed or (b) keep trying to catch up, but never do, so you're robbed of any satisfaction for your efforts. *SPEED CLEANING* allows you to do the cleaning well and to do it as quickly as humanly possible. *It will give you back your weekends.* You can reclaim time for other things that are fun, relaxing, or otherwise rewarding. And you can enjoy a clean house in the meantime.

A CATALOG OF PRODUCTS

Although *SPEED CLEANING* methods have stood the test of time, cleaning products change, are invented, and are improved continually. When *SPEED CLEANING* was first published, I started receiving letters (by the thousands!) from readers demanding to know: "So where's this fancy *cleaning apron* of yours?" and "I want to try some of that *Red Juice* you're so proud of." The Clean Team Catalog was created to satisfy those readers and to make professionally tested cleaning products available to consumers everywhere. The catalog has grown over the years, and we now test products from around the world to be able to offer the best homecare products available. If you would like to receive a free copy, please call us at 800-717-CLEAN (that's 717-2532), and we'll be happy to oblige. That telephone number is also a cleaning hot-line, so whenever you have a housecleaning question of any kind, call and we'll do our best to answer it.

A BIT OF HISTORY

Our method was developed by The Clean Team—San Francisco's preeminent house-cleaning service. For over eighteen years we've kept records of every visit to thousands of households in San Francisco. We used time-and-motion analysis and an endless comparison of cleaning products and equipment to develop a method that would save every step and every moment possible. The result is a thoroughly tested system of cleaning without a wasted motion. Besides being fast, we're very, very good: Our waiting list has, at times, been six months long.

SPEED CLEANING is a weekly cleaning system for areas that need attention every week or two: a thorough cleaning of the kitchen and bathrooms, including washing the floors in those rooms and dusting and vacuuming throughout the house. Our second book, *SPRING CLEANING*, covers the jobs that you don't tackle every time you clean but that you shouldn't ignore forever, either: jobs like washing windows and waxing floors. Daily cleaning tasks and household organization is the subject of our third book, *CLUTTER CONTROL*. It provides instruction on organizing cupboards, drawers, closets, magazines, and much more. Book four, *TALKING DIRT*, answers the 157 most frequently asked cleaning questions we've collected over the last ten years.

Because of our professional experience, we get to be The Boss for the time being. Maybe you'll develop your own system someday or customize ours for your own situation, but for now we're going to relieve you of the burden of making decisions. No arguments. No discussions. No compromises.

We clean over 18,000 times a year. Our three-person team can clean an average house in 42 minutes—start to finish! A one-bedroom apartment takes about 18 minutes! Believe it. And now we're going to show you how. Good luck, and have some fun with the time you save.

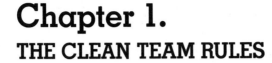

Chapter 1.
THE CLEAN TEAM RULES

Here are our trade secrets. We observe every one of them. Every day.

1. **Make every move count.** That means work around the room once. Don't backtrack. It also means you must carry your equipment and supplies with you so you don't make dozens of aggravating trips back and forth across the room. Walk around the room once and you're done, except for the floor.

2. **Use the right tools.** Ah! Here's probably the major timesaver of the bunch. Give your specialized gadgets to your enemies. You need real tools that cut time to shreds. Most of all, you need a *cleaning apron* to hang tools on and store cleaning supplies in as you move around the room. The method depends on it, and soon you'll feel lost without yours. If you don't have one, we'll tell you how to get one later in the book (page 191).

3. **Work from top to bottom.** Always. Period. Don't argue.

4. **If it isn't dirty, don't clean it.** For example, vertical surfaces are

almost never as dirty as horizontal surfaces. Upper shelves and molding have less dust than lower ones. Often all that's dirty about a surface is a few fingerprints, so don't clean the whole area.

5. Don't rinse or wipe a surface before it's clean. You'll just have to start over. In other words, when you're cleaning a surface, don't rinse or wipe just to see if you're done. If you were wrong, you'll have to start all over again. Learn to check as you're cleaning by "seeing through" the gunk to the surface below. Then you can tell when it's dislodged and ready to be wiped or rinsed . . . *once*!

6. Don't keep working after it's clean. Once you've reached ground zero, *stop*! You're cutting into VLT—Valuable Leisure Time. Rinse or wipe and move on.

7. If what you're doing isn't going to work, then shift to a heavier-duty cleaner or tool. You're going to get very good at knowing what tool or product to use without having to throw everything in the book at it. You'll be learning to anticipate what to reach for *before* you start a task so you won't have to shift.

8. Keep your tools in impeccable shape. Dull razors scratch—they don't clean. Clogged spray bottles puff up and make funny noises—they don't spray.

9. Repetition makes for smoother moves. Always put your tools back in the same spot in your apron. You can't spare the time to fumble around for them. And you can't afford to leave them lying around in alien places for the dog to carry away. You'll quickly get so expert you'll become aggravated if the tool you expected isn't in the right spot when you reach for it. Progress, progress.

10. Pay attention. Almost everything else will fall into place if you do. Don't think about the revisions in the tax code. Or anything else. In Latin: *Age quod agis*—"Do what you are doing."

11. Keep track of your time. Get a little faster every time.

12. Use both hands. Your work force is half idle if one hand is doing all the work. Finish one step with one hand and start the next step with the other. Or, wipe with one hand while the other steadies the object.

13. If there are more than one of you, work as a team. You're what the biologists call a "superorganism." If your partner gets done ten minutes faster, the *team* gets done ten minutes faster. And that is a wonderful thing. You can't stop being vigilant for one moment about what will speed up or slow down your partner's progress.

That's it. Like any new skill, Speed Cleaning must be learned, practiced, reviewed, and perfected. It's worth it. The payoff is that you will save hours every week. Hours that add up to days that you will spend *not* cleaning the house.

These are the basics. The rest of the book consists of specialized sections on tools, products, and jobs. Read the following chapter on tools and products. After that, if you're going to clean the kitchen, you are the "Kitchen Person," and so you should read the kitchen chapter next. The "Bathroom Person" and "Duster" should read the bathroom chapter and the dusting chapter respectively. If you are working alone, read the kitchen chapter after Chapter 2 (Tools and Supplies) and take a break before reading on.

Chapter 2.

TOOLS AND SUPPLIES

There are tools and supplies needed to do the job of cleaning that are indispensable. If you don't have them, you're going to have to get them—that's all there is to it—even though you may have been getting along without some of them for years.

After you're equipped with the proper products, guard against the entire Speed Cleaning process being slowly sabotaged because of tools wearing out or supplies running low. We're offering you time to spend *not* cleaning. Get and keep the right supplies and tools.

The strict rules you have learned about cleaning also apply to storing your cleaning supplies. Your tools are too important for you to have them scattered around the house where they could be lost, damaged, or not available when they are needed. If you are going to clean your house in 42 minutes, you can't spend 22 minutes gathering your supplies. We'll tell you where each item is stored and who uses it in the kitchen, bathroom, and dusting chapters.

Remember we're talking about speed, and the products we recommend offer speed while maintaining high quality. We appreciate the fact that there are premium products that we don't mention (e.g., fine paste waxes), but our job is to teach you speed. These are the products we use. We recognize that our method works best when you have access to the same products that we use. You can order just about everything we mention—including professional formulas—through our mail-order catalog (see page 191). At the same time, our system isn't so specific that you must use these very products. That wouldn't be fair. So we'll describe the products as well as possible so you can substitute others at your discretion. Occasionally we also list alternative retail brand names, but we do not necessarily endorse the effectiveness of those products.

Finally, if you're concerned about the environmental impact of the products you use, read Chapter 13 of this book before making your final choices.

Cleaning apron. Nothing makes sense in this system without an apron. It saves more time than all the other products combined. It carries the supplies and tools that allow you to "walk around the room once and you're done" (see Rule 1). If you're mad at having to wear one, especially with all this stuff packed into it and dangling from it, go ahead and have your tantrum. Then get over it. *Wear it when cleaning—start to finish.*

The Clean Team uses our own special aprons (see page 191) featured in the illustrations of this book. You can make your own apron, too: Just be sure it has lots of pockets for your tools, loops for your Red

and Blue Juice, and will tie securely around your waist. Wear it every time you clean!

A smart way to tie the apron on is to put it on backward, tie it, and turn it around. The Clean Team apron has seven pockets, three of which are dedicated to the following tools:

Toothbrush. Actually not recommended for your teeth at all, but it's the handiest brush we've seen for getting into tight places fast—like the areas around faucet handles, tile grout, impossible nooks and crannies on stovetops, light switches, etc. You'll be amazed at how often a spot will not respond to wiping but will come right up when agitated with a brush and a cleaning agent like Red Juice. This is a serious cleaning tool—not an old toothbrush.

Razor-blade holder. It's great for soap scum on shower doors, paint splatters on glass, and baked-on food on oven windows and surfaces of appliances. The one we use has a three-position blade for added safety.

Scraper. Occasionally you will encounter mysterious globs that are difficult to remove with the toothbrush—like petrified lumps of pancake batter or squished raisins. They can be removed in seconds with a scraper. We use a 1½-inch-wide steel spatula with a plastic handle.

A fourth pocket is used as a temporary storage for debris you encounter while cleaning. This saves extra trips to the trash. Use a gallon-size Ziploc storage bag as a liner and heavy duty paper clips (as shown) to keep it in place.

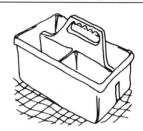

Carryall tray. Permanent storage for cleaning supplies.

Red Juice (in a spray bottle). Heavy-duty liquid cleaner. Professional cleaners call it "Red Juice" because the commercial concentrate often is red. Retail products include 409, Fantastik, and similar spray-on liquid cleaners. For simplicity's sake, we're going to call it "Red Juice" in this book. Use it for spray-and-wipe jobs except glass.

Blue Juice (in a spray bottle). Light-duty liquid cleaner. Similarly, most professional light-duty liquid cleaners happen to be blue. Consumer products include Windex or any similar liquid cleaner. Use it to spray and wipe mirrors, window glass, and picture glass.

Bleach (in a spray bottle). Use it to remove mold and mildew in the bathroom. Clorox is the most effective brand.

Spray bottles (three of them). Use them for Red Juice, Blue Juice, and bleach. Our model has a handle that fits well on the apron loops. Adjust the spray by turning the nozzle. If it won't spray easily, clean

the end of the tube inside the bottle with your toothbrush, or force water through it backward.

Tile Juice (in a squirt bottle). Liquid tub, shower, and tile cleaner. Use it to clean soap scum and mineral buildup from the tub/shower area.

Squirt bottle. Use it to apply Tile Juice. Any tile cleaner you purchase should already be in a container like this.

Feather duster. We are well aware of the purists who insist that feather dusters only move the dust around and don't get rid of it. We agree wholeheartedly that dust does need to be controlled in the home as much as possible. In some cases, this can mean wiping the dust up with furniture polish and a cloth, or washing baseboards, or vacuuming shelves. However, when maintaining a basically clean home on a regular basis, moving a small amount of dust very quickly from one (higher) level to another (lower) level where most of it is vacuumed away is a decidedly good thing. And a good feather duster happens to do this better than anything else. Get an air purifier if you are kept awake at night wondering what happened to all the dust.

The only feather duster that works is made with real feathers—ostrich down to be exact. Down feathers are full, soft, and almost spiderweblike at the ends. The feather duster we use is 18 inches long (including the handle). They're expensive and they're worth it. When you cut your cleaning time in half, you'll appreciate how valuable they are.

Cleaning cloths. The best are pure cotton—white only. Used table napkins are perfect. You may be able to find them at a local linen service. Don't substitute! Retire those old T-shirts, underwear, socks or hosiery, sheets, and most especially newspapers. Trying to use them to clean will make work and waste time. Keep a supply large enough that you will not run out once you've started to clean. When they are too worn for general use, use them on the oven or other heavy-duty jobs and discard them. Notice that we call them "cleaning cloths" so as not to suggest they're in tatters. We use retired cotton napkins that show some signs of wear, but they stop far short of being rags. We wash them in hot water with a liquid detergent and chlorine bleach to sanitize them.

There are two other possible choices. The next best thing to cotton table napkins is 100 percent cotton unfolded diapers. (If you have trouble finding them, they are still in the Sears mail order catalog.)

The third alternative is paper towels. If you're going to use them, don't pinch pennies. The best brand is Bounty Microwave paper towels.

Whatever your choice, we will refer to them as "cleaning cloths" from now on.

① Fold in half ② Fold again ③ Fold top to bottom

This is how to fold the cleaning cloths so they fit correctly in your carryall tray. It's simple but important, so please do it right.

Pump-spray furniture polish. We like Old English, and the pump-spray container carries well in the apron.

Furniture polishing cloth. You know, those yellow things you see in the stores—but get the untreated ones if you can. Use only for furniture polishing—not with Blue Juice or Red Juice. Don't wash in the same load with cloths that have wiped up powdered cleanser. The cleanser can be absorbed by the polishing cloth and scratch furniture.

Powdered cleanser. We use Comet. Use it to clean inside tubs, sinks, and toilets.

One-pint plastic container. (What's left over after you've eaten the expensive ice cream.) Use it in the bathroom to help rinse the hard-to-reach areas of the shower.

Whisk broom. Buy one with plastic bristles. Use it to clean the edges of carpets, especially on stairs, and for generalized brushing chores (e.g., between cushions on the couch).

50-foot extension cord on a cord caddy. Use a round cord because it resists knotting much more than a flat cord does. The cord caddy saves lots of time by keeping the cord organized. One good knot can take as long to untangle as it takes to vacuum a whole room.

Toilet brush. We use brushes with stiff bristles to improve their scrubbing ability. Don't buy the brushes with bristles held in place by a twisted wire. They aren't worth the wire they're twisted in.

Tile brush. A large brush with stiff synthetic bristles. Used to scrub the tile and grout in the shower. Also used in the tub itself and in the bathroom sink.

White scrub pad/sponge ("white pad"). We use the one made by Scotch-Brite that has a white scrub pad on one side and a sponge on the other. Used when a clean cloth isn't strong enough.

Green scrub pad/sponge ("green pad"). Same as above except for the color. Use this pad *only* for cleaning the oven because it will scratch just about anything.

Mop. After years of searching and finally finding a great sponge mop, we've abandoned it in favor of something unique and much, much faster. A "Sh-Mop." A major new design in cleaning is rare, but the Sh-Mop folks have done it. The Sh-Mop uses a flat rubber surface (a full 8 by 15 inches) covered with a removable, reusable, and washable terry cloth cover. That's 120 square inches of scrubbing power on

the floor versus about 25 square inches for a sponge mop, so the Sh-Mop is three to four times faster than even an excellent sponge mop. It also gets the floor cleaner, reaches into corners better, and cleans under the edges of appliances. It can also clean your walls and ceilings in nothing flat, but that's another story. And since the covers are tossed into the wash after use, it's like having a new, sparkling clean mop each time you clean. It comes with a supply of three terry cloth covers.

Floor cleaner/polisher. We use Brite. The coating it leaves is water-soluble, so it doesn't build up over time.

Ammonia. Use *clear* ammonia. Never "sudsy" or "detergent." Used to maintain floors not suited to cleaner/polisher (above).

Oven cleaner. Easy-Off is the simplest to use, and it works very well.

Rubber gloves. Use relatively loose-fitting, heavy-duty gloves. The cheap ones rip immediately.

Vacuum cleaner—canister type. (The "Big Vac.") You don't have to go buy one if you don't have this type already. But next time you buy a vacuum, this is the one to get. It's easy to maneuver, it has a second motor in the beater head, and it quickly separates so the hose can be used for other tasks as the need arises.

Vacuum cleaner—portable. (The "Little Vac.") This second vacuum is necessary if you're going to work in a team because you will often need two vacuums going at the same time. This is especially true if you have hardwood floors anywhere in the house.

Miscellaneous. Pliers, a multipurpose screwdriver, and a spare vacuum and bag for the Big Vac. Once you are on the job, you can't waste time looking for anything to solve little breakdowns.

Chapter 3.
THE KITCHEN

Stock your carryall tray with the following items:

1	can of powdered cleanser
1	spray bottle of Blue Juice
1	spray bottle of Red Juice
1	white scrub pad/sponge combination (white pad)
1	green scrub pad/sponge combination (green pad)
1	pad of No. 000 steel wool
1	feather duster
1	whisk broom
1	oven cleaner
1	pair of rubber gloves
1	bottle of floor cleaner/polisher (or ammonia)
10	cleaning cloths (folded)
3	terry cloth Sh-Mop covers

Stock your cleaning apron with:

1	scraper
1	toothbrush

   1   razor-blade holder with a sharp blade
   2   plastic bags (as liners) with clips

Hand-carry:

   1   Sh-Mop or your choice of mop

This chapter is designed to teach you how to clean any kitchen quickly, easily, and efficiently.

The Starting Point

Lean your Sh-Mop just inside the door. Put your carryall tray on the countertop just to the right of the sink. The strategy for cleaning this room is to work around the room clockwise, cleaning as you go—never backtracking, carrying all the tools and cleaners necessary in your apron.

This room is cleaned with lots of "pick up and replace" motions. For example, pick up your feather duster, use it, replace it; pick up the Red Juice, spray and wipe, replace it; pick up your toothbrush, etc. And when we say "spray and wipe," we mean that you'll be using a cleaning cloth and the Red or Blue Juice. These motions will become smooth and effortless with practice. We've picked your starting place for you: where you put your tray.

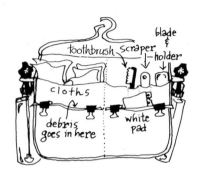

We've drawn the floor plan for a sample kitchen and shown your trajectory through the room. "S" is where you start, and your path is indicated with arrows. It's a good idea to draw your own kitchen floor plan after you've read this chapter. It will help you visualize your proposed cleaning trip around your kitchen and especially will help you to decide when to clean something in the middle of the room (like a worktable, for example).

Getting Dressed

Tie your apron around your waist tightly. Check to be sure that the toothbrush and other tools are in their proper pockets. Hang the Blue and Red Juice by their handles on your apron loops on the appropriate side. By "appropriate" we mean that if you put the Blue Juice on the left side, then *always* put it on the left side. This is so you can quickly reach for your Red or Blue Juice without stopping to see which is which. It saves time. The tops of the spray bottles have an annoying tendency to come loose at the worst possible moments, spilling the contents everywhere. Avoid this potential catastrophe by automatically tightening the tops when you first pick them up. Stick your feather duster in your back pocket. Put a whisk broom in your other back pocket. Use it to brush dirt out of vents, corners, and away from walls and appliances that the vacuum doesn't reach. Estimate the number of cleaning cloths you'll

Our kitchen:

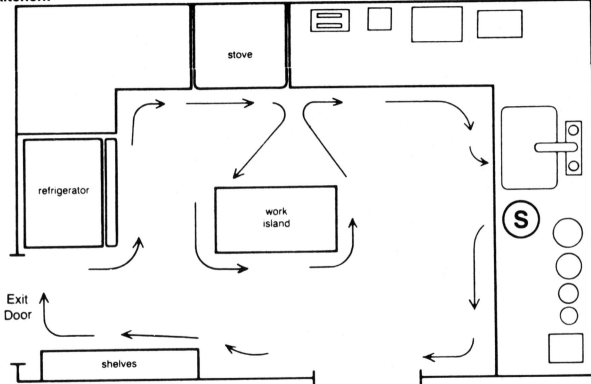

need and transfer them from the tray to your apron. At first, just guess by grabbing eight to ten cloths; as time goes on, you'll know how many you use. Finally check the illustration of you and your fully loaded apron. You're ready to move on.

Setting Up

Put any trash containers just outside the door or in the doorway, making sure they are out of the way (as much as possible) of the person who will be vacuuming. (Follow these directions even if you're working alone, since it is work you will do later and you want these items out of your way now.) Also, lay any throw rugs outside the door *flat* on the floor or carpet. That's *flat:* F-L-A-T. Flat. No corners tucked underneath. No rumpled mess. You're expecting the vacuumer to do the rug, so you'd better not make him or her stop to flatten it if you want to avoid a brawl in the hallway. Similarly, the person collecting the trash is not going to take the time to rummage around the kitchen on your behalf. That's your job as the Kitchen Person. If you save someone else on the team a step, you're saving yourself a step, and you're all going to the movies that much sooner. That's the idea.

Cupboards and Counters and Fingerprints

You are now going to start cleaning your way around our sample kitchen, *moving to the right, working from high to low* as you go. Above the counter are cupboards, and, since they are the highest, start with them. Usually all you have to clean are the fingerprints near the handles. Fingerprints need Red Juice, so grab your spray bottle from your apron loop and spray the prints lightly. Replace the spray bottle on your apron loop as you wipe the area dry with your other hand.

You will generally be using two cloths. Carry the drier cloth over your shoulder so it's easy to reach. When that cloth gets too damp for streakless cleaning (chrome fixtures, glass, etc.) but is still usable for general wiping, keep it in the apron pocket between uses, and sling a new dry cloth from your apron supply over your shoulder.

Cleaning fingerprints is a task where we are careful to apply Rule 4: "If it isn't dirty, don't clean it." If all you need to do is remove a fingerprint or two from an otherwise clean cabinet door, just spray the prints and wipe dry. Takes about five seconds. Don't haphazardly spray a large area of the cabinet door (which takes longer) and then have to wipe this larger area dry (which takes longer still). You've forgotten that all you wanted was that fingerprint and now you're cleaning the entire door. Stay focused on what you're doing, which is only the five-second job of a quick spray-and-wipe of a few fingerprints.

The places that often *don't* need cleaning are the vertical surfaces of the kitchen (the front of the cabinets, for example). The horizontal surfaces like the flat top of the counter will need cleaning every time. We have Newton to thank for this principle, plus his falling apple, gravity, and such. We are not proposing an excuse to be lazy or to skip things that need to be cleaned. Rather, the idea is to learn to be fast and efficient and aware of what you are doing. That includes *not* cleaning clean areas. After the fingerprints on the cabinet door, wipe the wall between the cabinets only if it has splatters. Otherwise it's not dirty, so don't clean it.

Spray and wipe the countertop area in front of you. (Pick up your carryall tray, spray and wipe the counter underneath it, and replace the tray.) Work from back to front, moving items to clean beneath and behind them. The "items" we're talking about are the sugar, flour, and tea canisters, the toaster, the food processor, and so forth. The spice rack may get moved to dust *behind* it, but that's all. Dealing with those individual containers is not light housecleaning, so just hit at the spice containers with your feather duster and save cleaning each spice bottle until some night you feel like doing it in front of the TV. Besides, the easiest way to clean a spice rack is to throw out all the old spices.

When moving items on the counter, move them straight forward just far enough for you to wipe the counter behind them. Before you move these items back into place, now is the time to dust or wipe them. Dust them if that is all they need since that is the faster operation. Now move them back and continue on down to the drawers below.

Be sure to dust or wipe the tops of the drawer fronts as you come to them. Always check drawer handles and knobs for fingerprints (same rule as above, for cabinet doors).

The drawer knobs or the cabinet handles are often easier to clean by using your toothbrush in the tight areas rather than by trying to fit your cleaning cloth into a small or awkward place. The toothbrush is in your apron and is perfect for corners and other areas difficult to clean with a cloth alone. Use the toothbrush and your Red Juice, and then wipe dry. After you've cleaned them with the toothbrush, a quick wipe with a cloth will suffice for many future cleanings.

As you work your way around the kitchen, you will do a lot of spraying and wiping, spraying and wiping. Usually you can do this with the spray bottle in one hand and a cloth in the other.

When cloths get too wet or soiled, put them in the plastic-lined pocket. Or throw them to your tray if you're a good shot. But be careful: Cloths soaked with Red Juice or almost any other cleaner may leave spots on the floor.

Get in the habit of always putting the spray bottles back in your apron loops, *not on the countertop.* We know it seems faster to leave them on the countertop, but it isn't. This may seem awkward at first, but do it—it's faster and it saves time.

Countertop Problems

So here you are, cleaning the counter with malice toward none and a song in your heart. Then you discover remnants of: (a) Saturday night's failed soufflé, (b) Sunday morning's blueberry pancake batter, and (c) other assorted stone artifacts that were once food. You are not amused. You took neither Chemistry nor Advanced Blasting Techniques in college. More to the point, you discover that when you spray and wipe these globs once, little or nothing happens. What to do?

First of all, when you come to a little nightmare on the countertop you have to resort to tools with greater cleaning power. Use your cleaning cloth most of the time since it normally will clean the countertop as it wipes up the Red Juice. When you encounter pockets of resistance like dried-on food, just move up to the tool of next magnitude—your white pad.

The white pad should be in your apron in a pocket lined with a plastic bag. When finished, always replace it in the same lined pocket. It doesn't matter that it gets dirty and begs to be rinsed, because you use it just to loosen dirt and not to remove it. Unless you just can't stand it anymore, don't rinse it until you get to the sink. Do try to get used to its being full of gunk.

Spray with Red Juice and agitate with the white pad until a mess of Red Juice and reconstituted five-day-old vegetable soup appears. This is the mess you need to learn to "see through" (Rule 5). To do this you have to learn how to tell how the counter feels when you've cleaned through the goop to the surface without rinsing or wiping to take a look. If you have difficulty judging when you have scrubbed down to the actual bare surface (without wiping), try spraying a little Red Juice on a clean counter area next to the dirty area you are cleaning. By first rubbing your white pad on the clean area and then the dirty area, you quickly learn to tell the difference by touch alone.

Another example of switching to a higher-horsepower tool is when you encounter food dried so hard that even a white pad takes forever to work. Let's say drips of pancake batter have dried to malicious little bits of stone stuck to the counter. When you tried your white pad, you found that you were rubbing one micron or so off the top of the dried pancake batter every swipe. You were using up MGT—Movie Going Time—again. When you first encounter the problem, better to put your cloth away, grab your scraper, and scrape the batter loose in a second or two. Replace the scraper and continue along your way. Be careful not to scratch the surface: Spray the surface first and keep the blade at a low angle. Remember, increase the force or strength of the tool only as necessary (Rule 7).

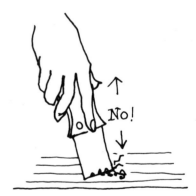

Picture Glass, Window Glass, and Mirrors

You need your Blue Juice and a dry cloth to clean these items, and since you are carrying them with you in your apron, there is no need to go back to the tray. To clean, spray lightly and evenly with Blue Juice and wipe with a dry cloth until the glass is dry. If you don't wipe it completely dry, you will leave streaks—and if you don't use a very dry cloth, you are wasting time since it will take you longer to wipe the glass dry. When we say spray lightly, we mean it. Glass or a mirror cleaned with a quick light spray of Blue Juice gets just as clean as a mirror drenched in it. It just takes two or three times longer if you overspray! So don't. Replace the Blue Juice sprayer after each use—back where it was on your apron loop.

Cobwebs and Doors

As you continue around the kitchen moving to the right, working from high to low, look all the way to the ceiling each time you advance to check for cobwebs. Spiders like corners. When you see a cobweb, grab your feather duster from your back pocket, mow down the cobweb, replace the duster, and proceed. If you can't reach the cobweb, use the detached vacuum wand as an extension for the feather duster.

You're now ready to pass a doorway in our sample kitchen. Another place to check for cobwebs as you pass by is the top of the door frame. Did you also check for fingerprints where people (especially very little people) seem to grab the door frame as they pass through? Good.

Open Shelves

Next are some shelves used to store cookbooks, pots and pans, and other kitchen stuff. Hit at the leading edges of these shelves with your feather duster only. (An alternative method is to clean thoroughly *one* shelf each time you clean the kitchen.) To clean a shelf, move all items to the right side and clean the left side, then move everything to the left side and repeat. Finally, redistribute the items as they were. Or, if there are too many things on the shelf, move just enough items to the floor or counter so there is space to move the remaining items. When moving items to the floor or counter, move them the least distance possible.

Refrigerator—Outside

Wipe the top first. Once you are cleaning this room on a regular basis, you may be able just to feather-dust the top, which takes only a second or two. If the top of the refrigerator is used as a storage area, then just dust around all the items up there and treat it like the shelf we just described.

Clean the fingerprints from the outside of the fridge—and there are

always some! Don't spray and wipe the entire refrigerator unless it needs it. Clean around the hinges and the nameplate of the refrigerator—your toothbrush is the best tool. Open the refrigerator door to wipe and clean the rubber gasket. If it is dirty, make sure to use your toothbrush here also. Once you get many areas like this clean, you won't have to do them again for a long time: e.g., the refrigerator hinges, nameplate, rubber gasket, and cabinet and drawer handles.

Wipe the refrigerator air vent (down near the floor) while the door is open—or if it is just dusty, use your feather duster or whisk broom. While the door is open, wipe fingerprints on top and on the side of the door near the handle. Also, clean off the line left by the gasket on the inside door lining. Check for easy or obvious little wipes that are needed on the visible areas of the interior shelves. Don't get carried away—it could take forever. (Instructions for a thorough cleaning of the inside of the refrigerator are in Chapter 8.)

The Stove Top

After you've cleaned the area above the stove—the hood usually needs to be sprayed and wiped—start at the back and work forward. Clean the vent filters by running them through the dishwasher occasionally. If they're gross or dilapidated, replace them. There are two main types of stove tops. Here is how to clean them.

Gas Ranges

These are easier to clean than electric ranges. Clean one side and then the other. First take the grates from the gas burners on the left side and set them on top of the grates on the right. Now spray and wipe the left side as necessary. You'll usually need your white pad here to get at the burned-on crud. If your pad won't work, use your scraper where possible, but the stove's curved edges often make this difficult.

If you are still unable to get the stove top clean, turn to your tray (next to the sink) and get your powdered cleanser. Use a tiny bit with your white pad. You will be using so little cleanser that you shouldn't even sprinkle it on the stove top. Instead, dab a bit from the top of the cleanser container with the wet edge of the white pad. If there is no cleanser on the top for you to use, then sprinkle a *small* amount on the stove top and dab with your white pad to pick up a little bit. As a last resort, use steel wool instead of the white pad. But take care not to scratch the surface.

After you have cleaned the left side, wipe (if needed) and replace the left grates, and then move the grates on the right side to the *counter* immediately to the right of the stove. Now clean the middle of the stove top and the right side, and replace the right grates. The grates themselves can be cleaned when necessary by putting them in the dishwasher.

a little pile of cleanser

Electric Ranges

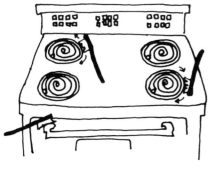

Usually there is a chrome or aluminum ring around the burners that needs attention. Normally you can clean around these rings (the edge of the ring where it meets the stove top) by spraying with Red Juice and using your toothbrush around each ring. Before you wipe, use your white pad to clean the metal itself. Now wipe dry with your cleaning cloth. As usual, work from back to front and from left to right. If necessary, use steel wool to clean the metal rings.

If you can't get the stove top clean without moving the metal rings, then go ahead and lift up that particular ring (only that one) and spray and agitate with your white pad and wipe. If there is an accumulation under the burner that must be removed (*don't* if it's not much), then pull the burner up, remove the drip tray, and dump loose debris into your plastic-lined apron pocket. Use Red Juice and the white pad or steel wool to quickly clean, then wipe and replace. Don't try to make this drip tray look like new: if it's hopeless, it's smarter to throw it away and replace it once or twice or twelve times a year—possibly with one of those nifty Teflon-coated pans. But they do get reasonably clean in the dishwasher, and you can use powdered cleanser to remove residual grime.

The Stove Front

Now that the top is clean, start down the front of the stove. The first little roadblock here is the row of burner control knobs. They can be cleaned by spraying with Red Juice and using your toothbrush on them and around their edges.

If you can't get this area clean without removing the controls, *first clean and wipe the knobs themselves while in place.* Then pull each one straight out, wipe it clean, and set it on the counter to the right of the stove in the same relative position it was in while on the stove. While the knobs are off, clean the area of the stove front you couldn't clean while the knobs were in place. Use Red Juice and white pad on this area and wipe it dry before replacing the knobs. This chore shouldn't have to be done often (unless the chef of the household is inclined toward hysterical flinging).

Open the oven door to get the oven side of the window. It can be cleaned with your razor blade. Be sure to spray the window first with Red Juice: It's easier to clean and it's also more difficult to scratch the glass when it's wet. This window should be cleaned even if you're not cleaning the inside of the oven. (Oven cleaning is the subject of Chapter 7.)

Wipe the rest of the front of the stove as necessary. Don't automatically clean the entire front of the stove. Remember that horizontal surfaces get dirty faster than vertical ones. Once again: If it isn't dirty, don't clean it.

The Middle of the Room

Now is the time we chose to turn around and do the work island in the middle of the sample kitchen. Not much to do here. Just spray and wipe the work space. The important thing is not to overlook it. Be sure to draw anything similar on your own floor plan and show by arrows when you are going to clean it.

Toaster, Toaster Oven, Can Opener, and Microwave

Return to the last bit of counter area to clean these items. You can make your ten-year-old toaster look like new by removing that burnt-on "brown" stuff with your razor *(gently)* and a white pad. Unplug the toaster and be brave. Wet the toaster liberally with Red Juice before you use the razor or you will scratch it. Just like the scraper, keep the razor at a low angle. Clean the rest of the toaster with Red Juice and your white pad, and use your toothbrush around the handles. Wipe the chrome dry and streakless (as you would glass). Clean the toaster oven similarly with Red Juice and use your toothbrush in those areas you are learning that your cloth won't reach. Also, use your razor blade on the (wet) inside glass of the toaster-oven door. Clean the can opener with Red Juice and use your toothbrush around the cutting wheels and gears as necessary. If any parts are removable, pop them into the dishwasher. The microwave is easy. Spray and wipe inside and out.

A Little Reminder

Remember, don't "come back" to anything. Make sure everything has been attended to the first time around. If you have to go back to clean something you missed, you are doing something wrong, and you are wasting valuable time better spent elsewhere.

The Sink

You will finish the trip around the kitchen by ending up in front of the sink. If there are dishes in the sink, there shouldn't be. That is not *weekly* cleaning. It is *daily* cleaning. The dishes should be put in the dishwasher or otherwise dealt with before you start this weekly cleaning.

Clean above the rim of the sink with Red Juice (not cleanser) and a cloth—all except in the bowl of the sink itself. Every time you clean, use your toothbrush around the faucets and where the sink meets the counter. It makes a vast difference and it takes only a few seconds.

Now use the powdered cleanser in the bowl of the sink. (Use powdered cleanser *below the rim only*, or you'll spend too much time rinsing.) Conveniently enough, the cleanser is in your carryall tray right next to the sink on the counter—where you left it when you started your trip around the kitchen. Wet the inside of the sink. Sprinkle cleanser lightly on the bottom of the sink, put the cleanser back, and then use your white pad to agitate the cleanser around the bottom and sides of the sink. Use your toothbrush to clean the little groove around the drain or garbage-disposal opening.

Rinse the sink thoroughly to remove the cleanser. Use your fingers to feel the sink bottom to be sure all the cleanser is removed. This is especially important since you may be using the sink as a bucket for some ammonia and water (see below) and some residual bleach from the cleanser could react with the ammonia. So rinse well. Now dry the faucet spigot and handles with a very dry cloth so they will shine nicely.

Put the Red and Blue Juice and the feather duster into your carryall tray. Take either ammonia or floor cleanser/polisher (see below) and put it in your apron pocket. Set the tray just outside the kitchen door (out of the path of the vacuuming).

The Floor

First step is to sweep or vacuum the floor with the Little Vac and its large brush attachment. Vacuum into the room so the cord or exhaust is not dragging or blowing debris. Pick up large items that may clog the vacuum—like dog or cat food, dried lettuce leaves, carrot slices, nylon stockings, sleeping hamsters, etc. Pay particular attention to corners and to the grout on tile floors. Use a broom if no vacuum is available. (It can actually be faster, unless there are lots of dustballs around.)

The next step depends on what type of floor you have. Use Method A (ammonia and water) if your floors are "no-wax" vinyl, hardwood floors coated with polyurethane, or tile floors (glazed, unglazed, or quarry). Use Method B (floor cleaner/polisher) if your floors are "wax" or "no-wax" vinyl or linoleum. (You may have noticed that "no-wax" vinyl floors made both lists. Use Method A or B on no-wax floors, or alternate between them.)

Grab the Sh-Mop from the doorway where you left it when you started the kitchen. Take two or three clean terry cloth Sh-Mop covers from your tray and put them in your apron. Put the bottle of ammonia or floor cleaner/polisher in your apron pocket, depending on whether you're using Method A or B below.

Method A. Ammonia and Water

Close the sink drain and run an inch or so of warm water into the sink. Then add a small amount of ammonia (approximately 3 table-spoons, depending on how dirty the floor is). Dip a Sh-Mop cover in this solution. Wring it out but leave it almost dripping wet, and place the cover over the Sh-Mop head. Start in the corner farthest away from the exit door and clean an area of the floor. When the terry cloth cover is too dry or dirty to continue, put the soiled cover into your lined apron pocket and dip a clean one in the ammonia solution in the sink. Repeat as necessary. As with other surfaces, different degrees of cleaning are called for: the dirtier areas of the floor in front of the stove, refrigerator, and sink require harder scrubbing than less-traveled areas. As you're mopping, be prepared to use your scraper to loosen mystery globs on the floor. Use the white pad to remove smears and heel marks.

Since you don't rinse the soiled terry cloth covers in the sink, the water in there stays perfectly clean. This means that a bucket is unnecessary, even for the most fastidious of cleaners.

When you pass the sink for the last time, let the water drain, rinse the sink, and dry the chrome if necessary. Mop your way out of the kitchen. Put the soiled terry cloth covers in the wash with the dirty cleaning cloths.

Method B. Floor Cleaner/Polisher

Close the sink drain and add just an inch or so of warm water. Dip a Sh-Mop cover into the water and wring it out a bit, but leave the cover almost dripping wet. (Or run a little warm water over it from the tap.) Put the cover on the Sh-Mop and go to the corner of the room farthest from the exit door. Apply a thin line of cleaner/polisher about 4 feet long directly to the floor. Don't apply closer than 2 feet to any wall or cabinet. Spread this line of cleaner/polisher as evenly as possible over an area of floor approximately 4 feet by 6 feet, using enough pressure to clean as you go. Your purpose is to use the Sh-Mop to pick up the dirt while leaving a little cleaner/polisher for a modest shine.

When using your scraper on blobs that the Sh-Mop doesn't remove, loosen them (once again at a low angle) and then either mop them up or pick them up and deposit them in your apron pocket. Sprinkle a little more water on the terry cloth cover as needed. Use the cover until it is too heavily soiled. Then put it into your lined apron pocket, moisten a fresh cover, and continue. When you pass the sink for the last time, let the water out, dry any water spots on the chrome, and clean your way out of the kitchen. Put soiled terry cloth covers into the wash with your cleaning cloths. Don't let them dry out before washing because most cleaner/polishers dry as hard as old paint. If it's going to be a while before you wash them, rinse the cleaner/polisher from the covers now.

If you have one of the shiny floors that tend to show streaks (marble, wood, smooth vinyl, for example), you can eliminate the streaks by drying the floor quickly with your Sh-Mop. Do this with a clean and *dry* terry cloth cover. Because the Sh-Mop has such a large surface area, it takes just a minute. And it works amazingly well—just as if you dried it with a towel on your hands and knees!

YOU'RE FINISHED!

If you're working alone, it's time to start the bathroom. If you're working in a team of two, report to your partner if he/she has finished the bathroom and begun dusting. If you have finished the kitchen first, then *you* start the dusting and give your partner a secondary assignment when your partner finishes the bathroom. (See Chapter 9, Team Cleaning.) If you're working in a team of three, go see the team leader.

On the next page is a summary of the kitchen procedures. You are most welcome to tape a photocopy of it at eye level in the kitchen to help you on your first adventure or two with Speed Cleaning your kitchen.

Kitchen Summary

(1) Lean Sh-Mop just inside door. Put tray on counter to right of sink. Hang spray bottles on apron loops. Put duster and whisk broom in back pockets and cloths in apron. Place trash cans and rugs outside. Spray/wipe around room to the right and top to bottom. When too wet or dirty, store cloths in plastic apron pocket or throw them into tray.

(2) COUNTER: Move items forward to wipe counter behind them. Dust/wipe items and replace. Use Red Juice and cloth, white pad, or scraper on counter.

( ) REFRIGERATOR: Red-Juice outside. Open door: Clean door gasket and air vent.

( ) STOVE TOP: Clean hood, then work from back to front with Red Juice and cloth, white pad, scraper, cleanser, or steel wool.

—Gas: Set left grates on right grates. Clean left side, and wipe and replace left grates. Set right grates on counter. Clean middle and right of stove top, then replace right grates.

—Electric: Try cleaning with toothbrush around burner with ring in place. If that fails, remove burner/ring assembly, dump debris into lined apron pocket, clean, and replace.

( ) STOVE FRONT: Try using toothbrush and Red Juice without removing knobs. If that fails, clean knobs in place, remove and wipe them, set them on counter, clean stove behind them, and then replace.

(6) SINK: Red-Juice rim. Use toothbrush around base of faucet. Sprinkle cleanser into bowl only and scrub with white pad. Rinse sink. Replace spray bottles and feather duster in tray. Set ammonia or Brite by sink. Set tray outside door.

(7) FLOOR: Vacuum with Little Vac or sweep. Fill sink with 1 inch warm water.

—Method A: Add 3 tablespoons ammonia. Dip Sh-Mop cover in solution. Wring but leave almost dripping. Put it on mop head. Start in far corner, changing covers as needed. Use scraper or white pad on problem spots.

—Method B: Dip Sh-Mop cover in water. Wring but leave almost dripping. Put it on mop head. Start in far corner, spreading 4-foot line of Brite for each 20 to 25 square feet. Change covers as needed.

Last time at sink, drain and rinse sink, polish faucet, and Sh-Mop your way to the exit. Put soiled covers in wash.

[NOTE.—Fill in Steps 3–5 for your own floor plan.]

Chapter 4.
THE BATHROOM

Stock your carryall tray with the following items:

- 1   can of powdered cleanser (with a plastic 1-pint container inverted over the top)
- 1   white scrub pad/sponge combination (white pad)
- 1   spray bottle of Blue Juice
- 1   spray bottle of Red Juice
- 1   toilet brush
- 1   tile brush
- 10   cleaning cloths (folded)
- 1   feather duster
- 1   whisk broom
- 1   spray bottle of bleach diluted one to four with water
- 1   squirt bottle of Tile Juice

Stock your cleaning apron with:

- 1   scraper
- 1   toothbrush
- 1   razor-blade holder with a sharp blade
- 2   plastic bags (as liners) with clips

Here is *your* bathroom. Looks a mess. Towels—some wet, some dry—in heaps everywhere. Mold growing in crevices. Toothpaste smeared on the mirror. Crud on the grout. Looks like a weekend job? The equivalent of three trips to the beach? Not at all! Eventually you'll be out of here in just 15 minutes or less.

The Starting Point

Walk into the bathroom. Do not be afraid. Face the tub. Put your tray down on the floor at the right end of the bathtub. The strategy for cleaning this room is to pick a starting point and proceed around the room clockwise, cleaning as you go—never backtracking, carrying all the tools and cleaners necessary with you in your apron and pockets. We've picked your starting point for you: where you put the tray.

On page 45 we've drawn the plan for a sample bathroom and shown your trajectory through the room. "S" is where you start, with arrows indicating the proper path to take. As with the kitchen, it's a good idea to draw the floor plan for your own bathroom.

Getting Dressed

Tie your apron around your waist tightly. Check to be sure the toothbrush and other tools are in their proper pockets. Hang the Blue

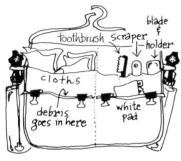

and Red Juice by their handles on your apron loops on the appropriate side: If you put the Blue Juice on the left side, then always put it on the left side. This is so you can quickly reach for your Red or Blue Juice without stopping to see which is which. It saves time. (Remember, the tops of the spray bottles have an annoying tendency to come loose at the worst possible moments, spilling the contents everywhere. Avoid this by automatically tightening the tops when you first pick them up.)

Don't put your feather duster or whisk broom in your back pockets or put cleaning cloths in your apron yet. In the bathroom, you'll be making two trips around the room instead of one: the first to do the wet work (the shower, tub, sink, and toilet), and the second to do the rest of the room.

Alert readers will notice that asking you to make two trips seems to be a violation of Rule 1. It is. Without going into a lengthy explanation, we're asking you to work like this in the bathroom (a) to avoid splashing previously cleaned areas, and (b) because you will be using brushes you normally don't carry with you. Don't think about it too much: just take our word for it.

Setting Up

Put any trash containers just outside the door (or in the doorway). Lay any throw rugs outside the door *flat* on the floor: no corners tucked

Our bathroom:

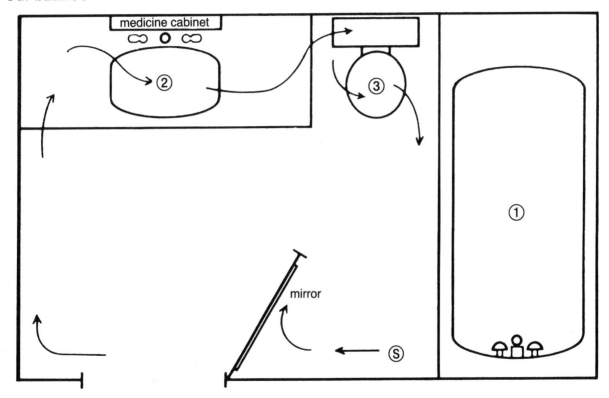

underneath. No rumpled mess. You're expecting the vacuumer (who may very well be you) to do the rug later, so make it as easy as possible.

The Shower Walls

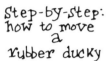

Step-by-step: how to move a rubber ducky

Set any items that are around the edge of the tub out on the floor. Whenever you move items like this, move them the shortest distance possible and keep them in the same relative position they were in. For example, if there is a shampoo container or a rubber ducky, move it straight toward you and set it on the floor in front of the tub. There are two reasons for doing it this way: (a) It is faster; (b) When it comes time to replace the items, you automatically know where they were. If there's a bar of soap, put it upside down on a folded cleaning cloth on the floor. (You're keeping the soft side up so soap isn't smeared all over.) Now that we've covered how to move a bottle of shampoo, a bar of soap, and a rubber ducky, let's move on.

First clean the shower walls around the tub—at least the areas that get wet when the shower is on. Wet the walls using the shower wand. Then use Tile Juice and the tile brush. (You have two brushes—one for the toilet and the other for the tub/shower and sink.) Although these are not in your apron, they are in your tray. And your tray (thanks to your observation of Clean Team Rule 1) is right at your feet. The Tile Juice is in a plastic squeeze bottle that squirts instead of sprays, so you don't have to inhale the fumes.

Most people's arms are long enough to reach into the tub enclosure to clean—and remember the brush adds more length too. So we recommend that you stand outside the tub to clean. An effective cleaner like Tile Juice liberates an extremely slippery layer of soap onto the tub floor. If you decide to step into the tub or shower to clean, at least make sure you are wearing nonslip rubber-soled shoes. And lay down a couple of cleaning cloths to stand on to make the surface less slippery. When you step out, step onto dry cloths so you don't slip or track Tile Juice plus gunk into the room.

Don't squirt Tile Juice in the areas that are already clean. (The higher part of the shower wall doesn't normally get wet during a shower and therefore doesn't need cleaning very often.)

Start by squirting some Tile Juice on the wall of the shower that is farthest from the drain, and use your brush to spread it around evenly. Don't scrub. Continue around the shower, squirting Tile Juice and spreading it around with circular movements of the brush. Just distribute the juice with the brush until you've covered the area of the shower wall that needs cleaning. Tile Juice works mainly by chemical action, so scrubbing is a waste of time at this point. It's got to sit there for a couple of minutes to loosen up the soap scum and hard water deposits. With the possible exception of the burned-on goop on the inside of an oven, there is nothing more resistant to cleaning than the hard water

and soap scum deposits that you encounter in an ordinary shower . . . so let the Tile Juice work for you.

If there are shower doors, continue applying Tile Juice on the inside of the doors after you've finished coating the walls. Replace the Tile Juice in your tray. Now start scrubbing the shower wall where you first applied the Tile Juice. The brush works much better than your white pad here because it digs into the grout between the tiles as well as the tiles themselves. Scrub in circles from top to bottom. Clean the plumbing fixtures as you come to them, using the tile brush (and toothbrush) as needed.

You'll be making a bubbly mess on the wall. Relax. It's just Tile Juice agitated by your scrubbing action, mixed with the soap and hard water deposits you are cleaning off. "See through" this mess (Rule 5) so you can tell when it's clean underneath and can quit cleaning one area and move on. You do this by learning to tell the difference between how your brush feels when it is cutting through the scum versus when it is down to the clean bare surface. One way to learn this difference is to scrub a clean tile high on the wall and then scrub a dirty one. Notice the difference in friction between the two areas as you scrub. Or use your fingers on the clean versus dirty areas to be able to feel the difference.

When you come to the soap dish, clean it with your toothbrush: First scrape off the soap that has collected in the dish with the *handle* end of your toothbrush. Now brush out the remaining soap with the bristle end. Use Red Juice only if necessary. Final rinsing comes when you rinse the tub/shower area.

Shower Doors and Runners

After you have scrubbed the tile wall, continue around to the inside of the shower door. Switch to the white pad for the shower doors, as it's more effective on this surface than the tile brush. (But only a white pad—never a green pad, which can scratch the glass.) If you have a shower curtain, skip ahead. (Don't try to clean it by hand: Throw it in the wash with a towel or throw it away.)

If the shower doors overlap, and you can't clean the area where they overlap by moving the doors, then spray some Red Juice on your white pad, wrap the pad around your scraper, and slide it into the gap between the doors. (If the white pad is too thick, use a cloth instead.) Now move the scraper up and down to clean this area. Be careful as you work that the scraper doesn't get exposed because it could scratch the glass. Next, remove the scraper and wrap a dry cloth around it for a final wipe. The reason you use Red Juice here instead of Tile Juice is that it's a difficult area to rinse, and Red Juice doesn't require the rinsing that Tile Juice does.

If there is anything like paint or those 1960s daisy stickers on the shower door that can't be removed with the Tile Juice and white pad, use your razor blade. Be sure that the blade is sharp, and use it properly (at a low angle), and you won't scratch the glass. And be careful not to nick the rubber gasket around the glass door.

It's still not time to rinse.

Next, take care of the shower door tracks (runners). Usually you can clean them with your toothbrush and Red Juice. If this doesn't work, use your scraper wrapped with a cloth. Move it back and forth inside the runner to clean it. Or fold your white pad in half and push it into the runner and move it back and forth. Again, *don't rinse yet.* There will probably be a lot of junk in the tracks, and the temptation to rinse repeatedly will be strong. Cleaning the shower runners is one of those jobs that's a mess the first time, so don't expect it to be perfect yet. It becomes less of a chore each time you do it, eventually needing only a quick wipe.

The Tub

Next is the tub—leaving the shower runners, the shower doors, and the shower walls clean but covered with Tile Juice and whatever ungodly mess you have loosened up—all *unrinsed.* We haven't forgotten.

Wet the sides and bottom of the tub if they need it. Get the powdered cleanser out of the tray and sprinkle it in the tub. Don't apply it anywhere but *in* the tub—not on the shower walls or faucets or shower head—just in the tub. Use the cleanser appropriately. If the tub isn't very dirty, don't use very much. While you are learning, resist your impulse to bombard the tub. Be conservative, since most powdered cleansers are abrasives and wear out porcelain. Also, it can take as much time to rinse it away as it does to scrub the whole tub. If you have a nonporcelain tub, use a specialty product instead of powdered cleanser.

Use your tile brush to scrub the tub, starting at the end away from the drain. Use the same "see through" method so you know when the porcelain under the foam and powder is clean. As necessary, use your toothbrush at the top of the tub where the tile meets the tub. This is often Mold Heaven (or Hell). It comes off rather easily if you can get at it with your toothbrush. The problem arises when it is found growing in the tiny cracks in the grout and can't be removed with your toothbrush. Remove what you can. Later you can use bleach on the rest, but not until you are just about to leave the bathroom, since chlorine bleach is obnoxious and you don't want to breathe it if you can help it.

cleaning between tile & tub

Rinsing the Shower and Tub

Now everything inside the tub/shower area is a clean but foamy mess, and you are ready to rinse. Put your *unrinsed* tile brush in the sink, and leave it there while you rinse the tub/shower area.

Turn on the shower to rinse. Use cold water so you don't fog up everything. If you are lucky enough to have a detachable shower head on a hose, rinsing is a pleasure. We happen to think that rinsing is a good enough reason to buy one . . . let alone being able to wash the dog with it.

Completely rinse the walls and doors before you rinse the tub. Rinse the shower walls from front (starting above the drain end) to back and from top to bottom. If there are areas that you can't reach with the shower spray, first try using your hand to deflect the spray to the area you need to rinse. If you still can't get it all rinsed, then use the plastic container that was over the top of the cleanser to catch water and throw it to those last nasty unrinsed spots.

After the walls are rinsed clean, rinse the tub—this time back to front toward the drain. *Use your fingers* to feel the bottom of the tub to know when all the cleanser is rinsed out. Don't depend on sight alone, as it is impossible to see a little leftover cleanser in a wet tub. The reverse, of course, is also true: If you leave a tiny bit of cleanser in the tub and wait for it to dry, it makes a powdery film that you can see halfway down the block.

After you have rinsed the tub and there is no leftover cleanser or Tile Juice, turn off the water. Don't replace the items from around the tub yet, because if there's any mold left you will spray it with bleach in a few minutes. But now is the time to wipe the chrome dry and shiny in the tub/shower area.

The Sink—Inside

Reach into the sink where you had set your tile brush. Wet the bowl of the sink. Since the brush is still full of cleanser from the tub, use it as is to clean the sink. Be careful to keep the cleanser only *inside the bowl* of the sink, since it is difficult to rinse away. *Never* let powdered cleanser get onto an area that is hard to rinse . . . especially the top ledge of the sink around the faucets.

When the sink is clean, rinse out your tile brush in the sink and put it away in your tray. Rinse out the sink. You haven't touched the sink rim or faucet yet because you will do that on the second trip around the room. Grab the toilet brush and cleanser from your tray.

The Toilet—Inside

Sprinkle cleanser in and around the sides of the toilet bowl. Wet the toilet brush by dipping it in the toilet and sprinkle some cleanser on it. Start high in the bowl, on the inside upper rim. Move the brush in a circular motion and clean as deep into the bowl as you can. The water will quickly become cloudy, so be sure to start at the top and methodically work your way around and down the bowl. Don't forget under the rim! All kinds of gremlins live there.

As you wash the toilet bowl, you are also washing and rinsing the toilet brush free of the cleanser you originally sprinkled on it. Shake excess water into the bowl and replace the brush. Flush the toilet. That's out of the way!

The Second Trip

Now it's time to clean around the room. Stick your feather duster and whisk broom into your back pockets. Estimate the number of cleaning cloths you'll need and transfer them from the tray to your apron. At first, try grabbing six to eight cloths. As time goes on, you'll know how many to use. You're ready to move on to the easy part.

You will generally be using two cloths. Carry the drier cloth over your shoulder so it's easy to reach. When that cloth gets too damp for streakless cleaning (mirrors, chrome fixtures, glass shelves, etc.) but is still usable for general wiping, keep it in the apron pocket between uses, and sling a new dry cloth from your apron supply over your shoulder. Throw your old cloth to the floor near your tray. If there's any danger of damage to the floor, put (or toss) the soiled cloths in your tray or you may ruin the carpet.

Mirrors

Start at the right of the tray, cleaning your way around the room, moving to the right and working from high to low. Be sure to close the door as you go by. There is often a mirror on the inside of the door, and it needs to be cleaned. You need your Blue Juice and a dry cloth to do this, and since you are carrying these items with you in your apron, there is no need to go back to the tray.

To clean a mirror, spray it *lightly* and evenly with Blue Juice and keep wiping with a dry cloth until the glass is dry. People who have trouble with streaks leave the mirror slightly damp. If you wipe completely dry, you'll eliminate streaks. Replace the Blue Juice sprayer after each use— back where it was on your apron loop.

Fingerprints

The door also may have fingerprints on it that need a quick spray-and-wipe. Fingerprints need Red Juice, so reach for it, spray the prints, replace the bottle, and wipe the area dry.

Here's a task where we are careful to apply Rule 4: "If it isn't dirty, don't clean it." If all you need to do is remove a fingerprint or two from an otherwise clean door, just spray the prints and wipe dry. Takes

about two seconds. Don't haphazardly spray a large area of the door (which takes longer) and then have to wipe this larger area dry (which takes longer still).

The places that often *don't* need cleaning are the vertical surfaces of the bathroom (the front of the toilet tank or the outside of the tub, for example). However, the horizontal surfaces (shelves or the top of the toilet tank, for example) will need cleaning every time.

Cobwebs

Train yourself to look all the way to the ceiling to check for cobwebs each time you advance. Spiders seem especially to like corners. When you see a cobweb, grab your feather duster from your back pocket, knock down the cobweb, replace the feather duster, and proceed. If you can't reach the cobweb, use one or two of the vacuum tubes as an extension wand for the feather duster.

Towels

Towel racks often need your attention—especially where the towel rack is attached to the wall. This is a place to use your toothbrush. A quick swipe with the toothbrush can clean such places much faster and better than your cleaning cloth alone.

Also clean the corners of the towel racks using your toothbrush and Red Juice, and then wipe dry. After you've cleaned them with the toothbrush, a quick wipe with a cloth will suffice for many future cleanings. Fold and rehang towels after you've finished with the rack.

The Medicine Cabinet

Wipe the very top with a cloth and then clean the mirror. If it has an outside shelf (usually with a supply of bathroom things on top of it—deodorant, toothpaste, perfume, etc.), move all the items to one side and spray and wipe the cleared area. (If the shelf is too crowded to merge the two halves, move the items to a nearby countertop.) Now pick up each item and wipe it clean as you move it to the other side. Then spray and wipe the second side, and finally redistribute the items as they were. Don't open and clean the inside of the cabinet itself, as that's not part of weekly cleaning.

Below the mirror you'll probably find the toothbrush holder. Clean it with a quick spray-and-wipe. To clean the holes in the holder, put a corner of your cleaning cloth through each hole and pull up and down a couple of times.

The Sink—Outside Only

When you come to the sink, use the Red Juice to clean around the faucets and the rest of the outside area of the sink—all but the inside of the sink itself (it's already clean, remember?). *Don't use powdered cleanser!* Use the toothbrush around the base of the faucets each time. Use your white pad and Red Juice around the rest of the outside of the sink. Then wipe as usual. Use a dry cloth for a final wipe and shine of the chrome sink fixtures. Don't dry the whole sink . . . just the chrome.

Debris

Check below the sink and around the cabinet for fingerprints. Continue around the bath to the right, working from top to bottom. Pay particular attention to plants (dust them and then remember to put the feather duster back in your rear pocket), windowsills, pictures, moldings, etc. Don't miss the light fixture in the middle of the room. As you encounter loose trash, dump the debris into the plastic-lined pocket of your apron. (Don't walk to the trash can.)

The Toilet—Outside

When you come to the toilet itself, start at the top of the tank and work down using Red Juice and a cloth. Once again, Clean Team Rule 4 applies: "If it isn't dirty, don't clean it." If the front of the toilet tank isn't dirty, don't take the time to "clean" phantom dirt. Don't forget to wipe the flushing handle as you go by.

When you get to the seat and lid, put them both in the "up" position and follow this sequence carefully. After you've done it a couple of times, you'll find that the explanation is much more complicated than the doing.

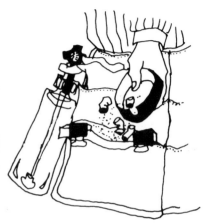

1. Spray the underside of the seat, and lower it.
2. Spray the top of the seat. Don't wipe yet.
3. Spray the underside of the lid, and lower it.
4. Spray the top of the lid. Also spray the hinges and the small flat area of porcelain on the far side of them.

Hang your Red Juice on your apron loop and wipe in the reverse order that you sprayed. That means you start with the small porcelain area and hinges. Now start using your toothbrush where needed. The first target is around those hinges. Then wipe the porcelain, the hinges, and the top of the lid dry. Raise the lid.

Use your toothbrush around the rubber bumpers and hinges (again). Wipe clean and dry. Be careful about splattering the clean porcelain. Wipe the top of the seat and raise it. Use the toothbrush again where needed and wipe dry. You're done with the lid and seat.

Now spray the top porcelain rim of the bowl. Tilt the seat and lid half forward with one hand and with the other retouch the hinge area of porcelain (catching any splatters). Push the lid and seat back fully upright and wipe the rim clean.

Clean all the way down the outside to the floor, using the toothbrush on areas such as where the toilet meets the floor and around those

use Red Juice!

annoying little plastic caps. (The inside of the toilet is clean, so don't touch it at all.) If there is mold left at the base of the toilet after you've cleaned this area, leave it and spray it with bleach later. You may very well want to dedicate a toothbrush exclusively for use in this delicate part of the bathroom ecosystem.

The Floor Around the Toilet

Even though you haven't started to clean the floor yet, we prefer to be on our hands and knees, eyeball to eyeball with the toilet, only once. So clean the (uncarpeted) floor around the base of the toilet while you're there. Spray the floor around the entire base of the toilet with Red Juice and wipe it clean and dry. Remember that you are throwing the cloths into the far corner of the room (or into your tray) as they get too soiled or wet. Also remember not to throw soiled cloths on carpets or wood floors—they might stain. If you have a carpeted bathroom, carry a whisk broom in your spare back pocket to brush the areas of carpet that the vacuum can't reach.

Shower Doors—Outside

Just before you finish your trip back to where you left your tray (on the floor at the right end of the tub), you will pass the shower doors.

wipe
wipe

Clean the *outside* only with Blue Juice. Often all you need to clean are the fingerprints around the handle. The outside of the tub occasionally needs a quick swipe. You're just about done!

The Floor

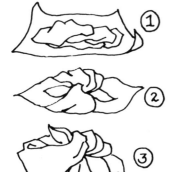

Take several fairly clean and dry cloths to do the floor. Go to the far corner and (on your hands and knees) start spraying and wiping with Red Juice as you back out of the room. The proper technique is to spray an area about 2 feet square lightly and evenly so that hairs and dust don't fly around. Then wipe up with your loosely folded cloths in a deliberate, methodical side-to-side movement (sort of a flattened "S" pattern). As you pick up hair and debris, carefully fold the cloth to trap the debris you've collected so far and continue. When one cloth is too dirty or full, use another cloth. You don't have to dry the floor, but wipe it and turn your cloths often to avoid making streaks.

When you come to the rubber ducky and bar of soap on the floor, you can put them back around the tub, provided there isn't mold left around the tub or shower. If there is, you'll treat it with bleach in a minute, so hold off replacing the ducky and soap until the treatment is finished.

After you've cleaned your way to the door, you can bundle the dirty cloths into a "ragamuffin" so you won't leave a trail of cleaning cloths and debris on the way to the washing machine later. To make a ragamuffin, spread one cloth on the floor and put the other cloths in the middle. Then tie opposite corners of the flat cloth together two at a time. Presto! A ragamuffin. And you're done with the floor.

Bleach

Now is the time to apply bleach to any remaining mold still clinging for dear life in the bathroom. First make sure the window is open. Bleach destroys just about everything, so treat it like strontium 90. Hold a cloth under the spray nozzle to catch any drips. Set the spray adjustment of your bottle to "stream" instead of "spray" so you minimize the amount of bleach in the air that you might inhale. Apply it as a liquid dribble directly on moldy areas. Wipe off any bleach that gets on the chrome fixtures immediately. Bleach dripping off chrome turns the tub's porcelain black. The discoloring isn't always permanent, but it can be awfully discouraging. When through, drape the same cloth over the spray nozzle to catch any drips as you take your tray through the house. One drip on a carpet will make a little white spot that lasts forever! Keep the top of the bleach spray bottle covered with a cloth at all times except when you're using it. Also aim the nozzle toward the center of the tray. Changes in room temperature can make bleach ooze out. So can pressure from other objects in your tray. The first time

you dribble bleach on your carpet, you'll realize we were not being too fussy, but it will be too late.

Escape

Replace the covered bleach bottle in your tray and set the tray outside the bathroom. It's not a good idea to leave bleach on surfaces for more than five minutes. Come back to the bathroom to rinse away the bleach. This will also give you an opportunity to admire your work.

After rinsing the bleach, replace the rubber ducky and all the other items you had removed from the shower and tub. If it needs it, redry the chrome quickly to put the finishing touch on the bathroom.

Don't move the trash or the carpet that you previously set outside. They will be taken care of after the carpet is vacuumed and it's time to empty the trash.

 **YOU'RE FINISHED!**

Spare Bathrooms

If there is a second bathroom that is used daily, go clean it now in exactly the same way. If there is a spare bathroom not often used, clean it according to the "If-It-Isn't-Dirty-Don't-Clean-It" rule and use only as much energy as needed. Don't automatically clean the mirrors if they're not dirty. Don't spray the door for fingerprints if none exist. Dust items that you might normally wipe. If the tub/shower hasn't been used, just wipe it quickly with a damp cloth, or spray and wipe with Blue Juice to remove dust. If you do this, it will be just as clean as the one that is used more often, but it will take you only a couple of minutes.

Different Bathroom Floor Plans

If there is a shower stall only and no tub, then treat the shower stall as you would the tub. In other words, set your tray by the right side of the shower when you first enter the bathroom.

If there is a tub separate from a shower stall, start by setting your tray down as we just taught you. Then clean the tub, the shower stall, the sink (inside), and the toilet (inside). Finally, clean around the room as previously discussed.

Bathroom Summary

(1) Put tray on floor at right end of tub. Put trash cans and rugs outside the room. Load up apron, but don't carry duster or whisk broom yet. Make two trips around the room: the first for Steps 2–6 and the other for the rest.

(2) SHOWER: Set loose items like soap on a cloth on the floor. Wet shower walls. Spread (don't scrub) Tile Juice evenly with tile brush starting with the wall farthest from the drain and ending with inside doors. Replace Tile Juice in tray. Start with first wall and scrub all surfaces with tile brush from top to bottom. Clean door tracks with Red Juice and the toothbrush or white pad.

(3) TUB: Wet tub and sprinkle lightly with cleanser. Scrub with tile brush, starting away from the drain. Put unrinsed brush in the sink.

(4) RINSE: Rinse walls top to bottom, starting near the drain. Rinse tub starting away from drain. Shine chrome.

(5) SINK (INSIDE): Use tile brush on the bowl. Rinse it and the brush and return brush to the tray.

(6) TOILET: Clean inside the toilet bowl with cleanser and toilet brush. Flush toilet and rinse brush. Put feather duster and whisk broom into back pockets. Add six to eight cloths to apron pocket. Start second trip around room.

( ) SINK (OUTSIDE): Spray/wipe faucet, rim, and front of sink. Shine faucet with a dry cloth.

( ) TOILET (OUTSIDE): Spray/wipe tank. Raise lid and seat. Spray underneath the seat and lower it. Spray top of seat. Spray underneath the lid and lower it. Spray top of lid and behind it near the hinges. Wipe in reverse order. Spray/wipe rest of toilet and floor near base. Continue your way around rest of room.

(9) FLOOR: Spray/wipe the floor with Red Juice and cloths, making large "S"-shaped movements from side to side as you work toward the door.

(10) BLEACH: Dribble bleach on areas that are still moldy after cleaning. Immediately wipe off bleach that dribbles onto metal surfaces. Rinse off remaining bleach with cold water in five minutes. Dry plumbing fixtures if wet. Replace soap and other items.

[Note.—Fill in Steps 7 and 8 for your own floor plan.]

Chapter 5.
DUSTING

Stock your carryall tray with the following items:

1	spray bottle of Blue Juice
1	spray bottle of Red Juice
10	cleaning cloths
	vacuum attachments
1	feather duster
1	whisk broom
1	50-foot extension cord (on a cord caddy)
1	bottle of furniture polish
1	polishing cloth
1	emergency kit:

      1 multipurpose screwdriver
      1 pair of pliers
      1 spare vacuum belt
      1 spare vacuum bag

Stock your cleaning apron with:

1	scraper
1	toothbrush

1   razor-blade holder with a sharp blade
1   plastic bag (as a liner) with clips

Definition

The Duster's job is to start cleaning the house except for the kitchen and bathroom. This work is drier than the work in the kitchen and bathroom: less spraying and wiping. There are several rooms involved, but they go faster, and there are no floors to wash—except wiping up an occasional drip of something. If you're going to work in a team, the Duster is also the team leader. But we'll get to that in Chapter 9.

Strategy

The strategy here is similar to the one for the kitchen and bathroom: Start in one place and then work your way through the rooms without backtracking, using The Clean Team rules.

As before, work from high to low. For the Duster, this instruction takes on additional importance: dust follows a relentless gravitational path downward, diverted only temporarily by air currents. Unless you have a healthy respect for this physical reality, you will find yourself redoing your work constantly. You will have an understandable human impulse first to dust what's right in front of you or what's interesting or what's easy to reach. Instead, train yourself to look *upward* toward molding, tops of picture frames, and light fixtures first, always checking for cobwebs.

Finish each area as you pass by. Do all the dusting, polishing, wiping, brushing, wet-cleaning, and tidying you need to do in an area as you pass through it. Change tools and cleaning supplies as needed: If you are dusting happily along with your feather duster and happen upon raspberry jam smeared on the top of the TV set, *quick!* Pop the feather duster into your back pocket with one hand as you reach for the Red Juice with the other. Spray with one hand as the other reaches for the cleaning cloth. Wipe with one hand as the other replaces the spray bottle on the apron loop. Then replace the cloth with one hand as the other hand reaches for the feather duster, and you are on your way again. A true blitz—a sign that you are mastering what you are doing. For pity's and time's sake, don't go around the room once to dust, once to polish, once to tidy things, etc.

Whether or not you are working with others, part of your strategy is to reduce the work load of the vacuumer. (The vacuumer will normally be someone else if you are working with another person.) Throughout this chapter, we'll suggest ways you can shorten vacuuming time by doing what would have been some of the vacuumer's work as you dust your way through the house.

Pay attention. Be alert to smarter ways of doing what you're doing.

When you shave off a minute or two each time you clean—not by rushing, but by smarter cleaning—that's what it's all about.

The Floor Plan

Since your home or apartment is unique, and since there are so many possible floor plans, we are going to discuss a typical one. Then after you've read this chapter, you'll draw a floor plan of your own home and chart your way through it. So before you even pick up your feather duster, you'll know where you're going to start, where you're going next, and where you'll finish.

First, though, we'll work our way through the rooms a Duster is likely to encounter—in this case, in our sample home. As we go, we'll explain cleaning methods and techniques to be used in each room and on the furniture, fixtures, and other items. Since there are so many possible arrangements, we do not suppose we're covering them all. We believe, however, that by learning our techniques for these typical rooms you'll know how to approach items not specifically mentioned here or items arranged in a different order in your home. We know this because it is much more important that you follow the *rules of cleaning* we're teaching rather than learn "hints" about specific items. You use the same technique on a $5,000 Baccarat crystal centerpiece as on a 50¢

Our floor plan:

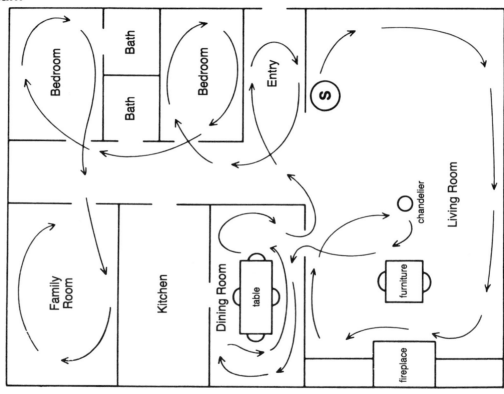

garage-sale vase. You may breathe a little differently, but you clean them the same way.

Our sample living room, dining room, entryway, and hall have rugs on a hardwood floor. The bedrooms have wall-to-wall carpeting.

Getting Dressed

Put your apron on and load it from your tray, putting Red Juice on one side and Blue Juice on the other. Put the furniture polish and polishing cloth in your apron. Put your feather duster in one back pocket and the whisk broom in the other. Take six to eight cleaning cloths and put them in the apron. (Next time you clean, you'll know better how many cloths to grab.)

Managing Cleaning Cloths

As you start to spray and wipe your way around the room, carry the drier cleaning cloth over your shoulder so it's easy to reach. When that cloth gets too damp for streakless cleaning (mirrors, picture glass, etc.) but is still usable for wiping, rotate it to the apron pocket and sling a new dry cloth from your apron over your shoulder. Use the damp cloth for wetter cleaning jobs like fingerprints, spots on the floor, and windowsills, for example. When that cloth in turn gets too damp or dirty and is no longer usable even for wiping, store it in the bottom of your lower right apron pocket.

Managing the Feather Duster

Approach most situations with your feather duster in one hand and the other hand free. Shift quickly to heavier-duty cleaning options as the situation demands, and gradually you'll notice you're beginning to do so smoothly and to anticipate your next move.

If you use proper technique with the feather duster, you will move most dust quickly from wherever it was to the floor, where it will be vacuumed away. (High to low—Rule 3.) Poor technique will throw a lot of dust into the air and contribute to the poor reputation unjustly suffered by feather dusters.

DEAD STOP!

Most dusting motions are fast, steady motions over the surface being dusted—a picture frame, for example. At the end of the dusting motion (i.e., at the end of the picture frame), bring the duster to a dead stop. *Don't let the feathers flip into the air at the end of a stroke, thereby throwing all the dust into the air, where it will stay until you've finished cleaning and then settle back on all the furniture you've just finished cleaning.*

By coming to a dead stop at the end of each stroke, you will give the dust a chance to cling to the feathers. To remove the accumulated dust from the feathers, tap the feather duster smartly against your ankle, close to the floor, every once in a while. The object is to get the dust to settle on the floor where it will await vacuuming.

The Starting Point

Set your tray on the floor next to the door of the first room you're going to clean. On our floor plan (page 71), the starting point is shown by an "S" in a circle. For our purposes, you're going to start by cleaning the living room.

The Living Room

Cobwebs

Rule 3 says to work from top to bottom, so the first thing to do is to look up and check for cobwebs. Use your feather duster to remove them. If they're out of reach, stick your feather duster in the end of one or two lengths of vacuum wand. Then do a quick tour of the whole room, as it's too time-consuming to put down and pick up this makeshift apparatus more than once. Kill all spiders. Or catch them and let them loose outside if you're a pacifist or if they beg for mercy.

Fingerprints

Dust door panels or trim with the feather duster. Clean fingerprints around the doorknob with Red Juice (spray and wipe). Then, with Red Juice and cloth still in hand, clean the light switch next to the door. Move to the right along the wall, dusting everything from cobwebs on the ceiling to dust on the baseboards with long "wiping" motions of the feather duster. Remember to stop dead at the end of each swipe. Shift to wet cleaning (Red Juice, Blue Juice, or polish) only if you need to—as Rule 7 says.

Mirrors and Pictures

Picture glass typically needs wet cleaning only a few times a year. To test for cleanliness, run your *clean* and *dry* fingers lightly over the glass. Any graininess or stickiness means clean it. If it needs it, wet-clean by spraying Blue Juice lightly and evenly and then wiping dry. Wipe it really *dry*, not just until it looks dry. The difference equals a streak: Glass begins to *look* clean as you're wiping it even though it's still slightly wet with Blue Juice. Wipe until it's completely dry. Trust us.

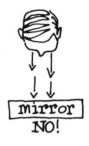

mirror
NO!

Wipe in broad movements, taking care to wipe the corners well. Don't wipe in small circles or random excursions. Also, stabilize the frame with one hand—*firmly*, don't be halfhearted—while you wipe with the other. If you don't stabilize it, it may fall or leave scratches on the wall from the frame jiggling as you clean it.

mirror
YES!

The woods are full of people who can do a slow and mediocre job of cleaning glass. Our goals are higher, and one of the things that makes the greatest difference is checking your work. If you look head on into the glass, you will see a reflection of your own sweet face, but you may miss 80 percent of the dirt on the surface. Check it from as narrow an angle as you can.

Once you have cleaned a picture frame or mirror, it probably won't need a thorough wet-cleaning again for weeks or even months. Dust it every week or so on the top of the frame and occasionally even the glass itself.

Wall Marks

As you dust, check the walls for marks and fingerprints. Use Red Juice on wall marks of all kinds. Before you move to the next section of the wall, look all the way to the floor (especially when there is a wood or tile floor) to check for little dried-up spills that should be wiped away.

End Table—Surface

Clean *above* the end table first. With wiping motions of the feather duster, dust the lamp shade, bulb, lamp, and then the objects on the table. The surface of an end table is rarely touched, so there is no need to use furniture polish every week. Just use your furniture-polish cloth without extra polish. By "polish" we mean either wax or oil—an important distinction to make, it turns out, as the two do not get along well on the surface of furniture. If you've been using an oil polish ("lemon oil," "red oil," etc.) continue using it. Otherwise use the Old English from your apron pocket—a type of liquid wax that we find very easy to use.

End Table—Objects

When cleaning an object-laden table, just work from top to bottom again. Use your feather duster first (on lamps and objects on the table), then a cleaning cloth (on objects that need more cleaning), and then the polishing cloth (on the table itself).

Use caution. Cleaning and moving small items on shelves and tables is the scene of most accidents for dusters. A few guidelines will avoid most accidents: most important, pay attention to what's in front of you. Use both hands to move anything top-heavy or irreplaceable, or anything composed of more than one piece (e.g., a hurricane-lamp base with a glass lantern on top). It's almost never wise to move something on a pedestal by pushing the pedestal. Steady the top piece with one hand and grab the pedestal with the other. You usually get to make only one mistake with such things. And keep a wary eye out for heavy objects: *Do not*, oh *do not*, slide them across the surface of furniture. Scratches will follow in their path without fail or mercy.

Dust Rings

Our end table is on a wood floor, so use your feather duster to wipe the floor around the legs and underneath it to save time for the vacuumer. By dusting these areas where the vacuum would leave rings

or where the vacuum can't reach, you are speeding up that job, since the vacuumer won't have to stop to do it. If furniture is on a carpet, use the whisk broom instead of the feather duster for this job.

Couch

Fabrics vary greatly in characteristics that affect cleaning strategy. If you're lucky, your furniture will need only a quick swipe with the whisk broom. At the other extreme are fabrics that hair will cling to until you pluck it off like a surgeon. In the middle are a great number of fabrics that will cooperate reasonably and respond to your whisk broom. Every so often even the most agreeable of fabrics could use a good vacuuming, however, to remove accumulated dust. The frequency of vacuuming depends on how dusty your environment is and how sloppy you are. If you like to eat crackers while sitting on your couch or if the cat sleeps there, you will overwhelm the capacities of the whisk broom and will have to call in the vacuum regularly. But not now. *First finish* dusting and polishing.

Back to our sample couch, however, which has pet hair and cookie crumbs on it. Clean from the top down, using your whisk broom. You will be tempted to start with the cushions, as they are easiest to deal with. Resist. First, starting with the left side of the couch, whisk the crumbs and hair from the top, back, and sides. (Careful not to make work for yourself by whisking debris onto the clean end table.) Whisk down and toward the cushion.

Should you clean under the cushions? Ah, the eternal question asked by reluctant cleaners! The answer lies under those very cushions. Lift up a cushion or two and peek. You will know instantly. If it needs a thorough cleaning underneath, set the left cushion on the one next to it to get it out of the way while you whisk out that area. Then move to the next section and (starting once again at the top of the couch) repeat the process. If the area under the cushions only needs a touch-up, just tilt the cushion up for a quick swipe with the whisk broom. Leave the tops of the cushion for the vacuumer, who can do them much faster.

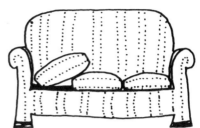

To signal the vacuumer that the cushion tops *only* are to be vacuumed, leave a cushion overlapping the next one. The large vacuum has a beater brush that is safe for most fabrics. You simply lift the beater brush up to the couch cushions and vacuum away. No further vacuuming is necessary as long as you have removed the hair and crumbs from the rest of the couch. Keep in mind that you want to do everything possible to make vacuuming easier. These steps greatly reduce vacuuming time.

Be careful. Vacuuming fabric with the beater brush can catch certain loose fabrics, can catch tassels or strings, can damage certain delicate fabrics, or may accelerate the wear and tear of your couch. If you prefer to avoid any risk, use the small vacuum.

If the amount of pet hair on the couch demands that the *entire* couch be vacuumed, then don't whisk it at all. It can be vacuumed with the small vacuum after the dusting. The signal to remind yourself or a

partner to vacuum the *entire* couch is to stand one cushion straight up.

To signal the vacuumer to clean *under* the couch, move one corner of the couch forward. If the couch is the sort that sits flush to the floor, it doesn't need to be moved often, since it's almost impossible for dirt to get under it.

Plants

Continuing top to bottom and left to right, you come upon a large potted plant in the corner. Dust the plant with the feather duster top to bottom. On broad-leaf plants, support a leaf with one open hand while you dust with the other so the stem doesn't snap. Pick up the dead leaves, which often clog the vacuum, and put them in the apron trash pocket. Our sample plant is close to the wall and too heavy to move easily, so, with a cleaning cloth, dust the hardwood floor around and behind it where the vacuum can't reach—once again, saving the vacuumer time.

Drapes and Window Frames

Next is a wall with windows. With your feather duster, dust the top of the drapes and curtain rods for cobwebs. Working from top to bottom, dust all the window frames. Don't use a feather duster on wet windows unless you want to ruin your day. (A wet feather duster is a pitiful sight.) Often in the winter you'll have to wipe with a cloth because the frames are wet. Then dust the windowsill.

Leather Chair

Particles of dust, sand, and grit work their way into leather and wreak havoc with the finish and stitching. The whisk broom is excellent for dusting leather furniture, especially if the upholstery is tufted and has buttons or piping. And use your toothbrush if the cracks and crevices are dirty: keep both in hand, because with the whisk broom you can brush away particles the toothbrush dredges up. (Brush/swipe, brush/swipe, brush/swipe. . . .)

Bookshelves

Next is the fireplace wall with bookshelves on each side. Dust the top of the books if there is room, and dust the exposed edges of the shelves with long wiping motions of the feather duster. Remember to shake the dust out of the feather duster at regular intervals near floor level by whacking it against your ankle.

Dust very ornate objects (e.g., candlesticks) with small squiggly motions of the feather duster so the feathers get into all the little places.

Do not dust the hearth, because you will get soot on your feather duster and ruin it. Leave it for the small vacuum. If the room had wall-to-wall carpeting, you would wipe the hearth with a cloth so the vacuumer wouldn't have to bring in the small vacuum just for the hearth. (See Chapter 6, Vacuuming.)

Middle of the Room

You've worked your way to the entrance to the dining room. Before leaving the living room, dust the molding on the small section of wall between the door to the entry hall and the door to the dining room. Move to the center of the room and dust the chandelier with the feather duster (squiggly motions).

Polishing the Table

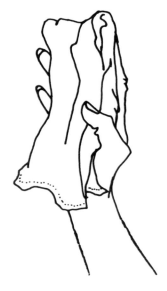

On the carpet in front of the fireplace is a card table with four chairs that have been well used. Moving around the table, first pull each of the chairs away from the table and dust each one in turn. Do this with your polishing cloth in one hand and a feather duster in the other. Use the polishing cloth on the tops and arms of the chairs and the feather duster on the frame and slats. Leave the chairs away from the table to make it easier for the vacuumer to maneuver.

To polish a small tabletop, spray on polish in a thin and even coat. Begin to wipe immediately, because polish left in place even for a minute or so begins to eat into the finish. (If that starts to happen, spray on more and wipe like mad.) *Wipe in the direction of the wood grain.* This is more shrewd than superstitious: Streaks left by imperfect polishing will be camouflaged by blending in with the wood grain if you rub in that direction. Wipe with your polishing cloth folded into an area as large as your hand—not mushed into a ball—so you make maximum use of each swipe. *(Saves time.)* As you rub, the polish will spread out evenly and begin to dry. When it is almost finished drying, flip the cloth onto its back—which should be kept *dry*—and buff the finish to a shine. Make big sweeping movements to save time. When the table exceeds your arm length, spray half at a time. (The table, that is, not your arm.) Don't press down hard as you buff: It's harder work and you can scratch the surface even with polish. Finally, check for streaks and missed spots, and deal with them with the driest part of the cloth.

Dining Room

Enter the dining room from the living room and begin dusting above the doorway, working from top to bottom as always. In the first corner is a plant: Use your feather duster as you did earlier.

Mirror-top Buffet

Across the back wall is a mirror-top buffet with liquor bottles on top. Move the bottles to the right side and spray and wipe the vacated area. Use a Blue-Juice-sprayed cloth to clean the bottles as you replace them. If you encounter cigarette butts or other debris, remember to deposit same in your apron trash pocket. *Do not* walk around looking for a trash can! Clean the other side of the mirror top and continue. Our buffet sits on the hardwood floor on short legs. The vacuum can get underneath, but use the feather duster around the legs to prevent dust rings.

Dining-room Table

Polish the dining-room table each time unless it hasn't been used at all. It saves the most time to polish half of the table, dust the chairs closest to you, polish the other half of the table, and then finish the chairs. The point is to minimize retracing your steps. A good brushing is all most chair seats need. Don't forget to dust the chair rungs or the legs themselves if they curve outward near the tip. While you're down there, check to see if either the pedestal or crossbeams of the table need dusting too.

The Hallway

Go into the entry hall and dust in the same way, beginning above the door and working from top to bottom around the entry. Our table is unused and requires only the feather duster for the objects and the polishing cloth for the table. Use the feather duster around the legs of the table again.

Enter the hall and continue in the same top-to-bottom manner but alternately dust and wipe sections of *both walls* as you move down the hall. Don't do one side and then the other; you waste time retracing your route.

The Bedrooms

Enter the first bedroom off the hall. Begin in the same manner, above the door, moving to the right. Pull the foot of the bed away from the wall to indicate that the vacuumer should clean under it this time. As the Duster, you are in charge of knowing which chores are to be rotated—and which rotation is to be done this time. An example is vacuuming under the bed, which may not need to be done every week but can't be ignored forever either. The same applies to heavy furniture (like the couch), and some high molding and other difficult areas to vacuum.

Desk

The desk in our sample room is so close to the corner that the head of the vacuum won't fit, so use the whisk broom to dust and fluff that section of carpet next to the desk. (Remember, this is wall-to-wall carpet.) This will keep the carpet pile from looking dusty. You can vacuum this spot every few months when you move the desk to vacuum behind it. Also, set any trash cans as close to the doorway as you can without interrupting your trip around the room.

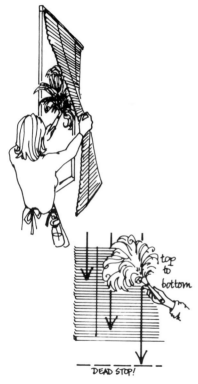

top
to
bottom

DEAD STOP!

Telephone

Only rarely can a phone be just dusted, as it is one of the most frequently used objects in the house. Clean it with the already-wet furniture polishing cloth. It's a mess to spray the phone directly, as there are all sorts of nooks and crannies. Only if the phone is extraordinarily dirty should you spray it directly with furniture polish and use your toothbrush to dislodge dirt from crevices. Unravel a tangled cord by unplugging one end and uncoiling it. To avoid leaving fingerprints, polish the body of the phone first and then the handset. Likewise, replace the handset not with your bare hand but with the polishing cloth wrapped around it. (It takes time for the polish to dry on such nonporous surfaces, during which time objects fall prey to fingerprints.)

Miniblinds

On the window are dusty miniature blinds. Lower them to their full length and turn the slats to the closed position so the blinds curve *away* from you. By grasping the string that runs through them, pull them away from the window so you can reach behind them with your feather duster. Dust them using long *downward only* strokes at a slow speed so the feather duster can do more dust-catching than dust-storming. Remember, stop the feather duster dead still at the end of each stroke. Remove the dust collected after each stroke by tapping the duster against your ankle near the floor. Now turn the slats forward so the blind curves *toward* you. Dust the front in the same long, slow *downward* motions.

The Family Room

This room is often full and well used. This makes it doubly important that you follow the Speed Cleaning method exactly.

The TV, the VCR, and the Stereo

The TV is cleaned by using a feather duster on the back and Blue Juice on the body and screen. Use your feather duster on the VCR. To remove fingerprints, spray Red Juice on your cloth and wipe them off. Make sure you don't get Red (or any other kind of) Juice anywhere near videotapes or the inner machinery of the VCR. Also use your feather duster on the stereo, being careful not to snag the tone arm or needle and thereby destroy the cartridge you just paid a day's salary for. Use your already damp furniture polish cloth to remove fingerprints from the plastic dust cover. Or spray it directly if it's very dusty to protect against scratching the soft plastic.

YOU'RE FINISHED!

It's not quite time for your nap yet—but it's getting close. All that remains is the vacuuming!

Things Often Overlooked by Distracted Dusters

- Windowsills and molding on windowpanes
- Baseboards
- Chandelier chains
- Hanging light fixtures, especially the bulbs
- Bulbs in table lamps and inside surfaces of shades
- Telephones
- Plants (dust broadleaf ones just like anything else)
- Backs of chairs
- Curved feet of chairs and tables
- Crossbeams underneath tables
- Heater and exhaust vents
- Tops of drawers and drawer pulls
- Tops of books on shelves
- Bottom shelves of anything, but especially end tables and coffee tables
- Areas around electric cords that trap circulating dust
- Drapes near the top
- Louvered shutters
- TV picture tubes

Chapter 6.
VACUUMING

There Are Two of Them

In a fair world you are part of a team and therefore need two vacuums, since the opportunity to save even more time justifies the expense. In an unfair world you have to get by with one vacuum. Let's assume it's fair for now and ignore the accumulating evidence to the contrary.

Their Uses

Use the bigger, canister vacuum ("Big Vac") on carpets, rugs, and some upholstery. Use the smaller, portable vacuum ("Little Vac") on hardwood floors, the kitchen floor, and all types of upholstery. If you don't have two vacuums, don't worry when we tell you to use the Little Vac for one task or another. You can use the Big Vac with different attachments just about as easily.

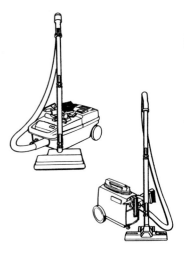

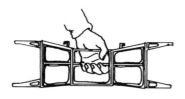

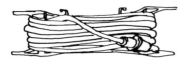

How to Vacuum with the Big Vac

The most important point in vacuuming is to follow Rule 1. Therefore, you plug the vacuum in once and then vacuum the entire house without ever replugging it. This little gem of an idea will save you 20 percent or more vacuuming time by itself. You'll never backtrack (sound familiar?) to first unplug and then go looking in the next room for another plug—which is often behind the TV or couch or in some other infuriating spot.

To accomplish this feat we use a 50-foot extension cord. Fifty feet should do it unless your home is very large. The cord is stored on a cord caddy that keeps it from tangling and tying itself into knots.

The ideal outlet is also as close to your starting point as possible while still allowing you to vacuum the entire house without replugging. This also means that most of the cord will be *behind* you as you vacuum, which is faster than working toward the cord. Take the time to keep the cord behind you and untangled.

Take the vacuum and extension cord (on its caddy) to your starting point. Unwrap the vacuum cord and connect it to the extension cord only after tying them together in a simple knot. This is important because it will keep them from pulling apart the first time you give the cord a little tug. Next, unwrap most of the extension cord in a neat circular pile that won't turn into a giant knot later. Unwrap and lay the last section of cord in a straight line to the electrical outlet you selected. The cord in front of you is in a straight line and is much easier to maneuver out of your way, since you can move it from side to side a few inches with the beater head of the vacuum without bending to pick it up.

The above applies to wall-to-wall carpeting without modification. If you have any exposed hardwood flooring, put the extension-cord pile on the hardwood floor nearest to where you will start vacuuming the rug. Otherwise you'd have to pick the pile up to start vacuuming.

Floors

Start vacuuming in the room where the Duster started, and work toward the right. Vacuum systematically, so you don't overlook an area or do it more than once. Usually you can do a living room in three fairly equal parts. Use furniture in the room as landmarks to divide up the room so you don't overlap or skip areas. Vacuum with one hand, keeping the other hand available to move furniture or other items out of your way.

Typical vacuuming is a forward and backward motion. Go forward one full length of the vacuum hose each time. Move sideways one full width of the vacuum head with each backward motion. Keep the canister part of the vacuum to your left as you vacuum the room to your right. Be very careful as you pull the canister, because if an accident

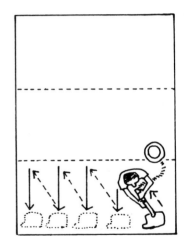

can happen it will. (If you're using an upright vacuum, move forward one long step and then backward one and a half steps, because your backward steps are shorter.)

If some areas to be vacuumed are well traveled and need extra attention, vacuum more slowly or repeat each push and pull of the vacuum. If an area is little used, speed up and don't go over it twice.

Furniture

The Duster has left you signals to save time. An overlapped cushion tells you to vacuum the tops of the cushions only. Just move your beater-bar from the floor to the cushion and vacuum away. This will not harm most fabrics. But don't use the beater on very loose-fitting fabric and be careful of tassels or loose strings. (Use the Little Vac instead.) A turned-up cushion tells you to vacuum the entire couch. You use the Little Vac to do this, so leave the upturned cushion alone since that will be done later. If your vacuum doesn't have a motorized beater head, don't use it to vacuum cushions or furniture. In other words, don't use a nonmotorized floor attachment, because it will transfer all sorts of fuzz from the floor to the furniture. The signal to vacuum the tops of cushions only is a single cushion left overlapping the one next to it.

The signal to vacuum under a piece of furniture is when it is moved out at an angle from its normal position. The vacuumer puts the furniture back in its original position afterward.

Moving the Furniture

The rule is to move the item as short a distance as possible: tip a chair back, for example, instead of transporting it. If you're helping by moving furniture as someone else vacuums, lift the furniture straight up, let your partner vacuum the area, and then replace it. If you're vacuuming on your own, you will have learned not to leave trays, mops, the Little Vac, trash, etc., in your direct path. Move one end of a table an inch or two to vacuum where the legs were, and then replace.

Only if you're working in a team, it's a good idea for you *not* to replace chairs and other displaced furniture. Better to carry on vacuuming and let someone else (or you) replace items at the end of cleaning. Vacuuming is often the longest job, and every step possible should be taken to avoid stopping once you've started. For example, when you reach a spot where the vacuum head doesn't fit and an Act of Congress is required to get it to fit—like moving a heavy plant, or a desk, etc.—then this area should already have been cleaned with a whisk broom, feather duster, or dust cloth.

Stairs

Start at the top and vacuum your way down. If you have a canister vacuum, set it six or eight stairs down from the top. When you've vacuumed down to it, move it down six or eight more steps. Use the whisk broom from your back pocket to clean out edges and corners of the stairs as needed. It's easy and fast. Whisk several steps and then vacuum several steps and repeat. Vacuum with back-and-forth motions of the beater head—not side-to-side. Do be careful as you vacuum backward down the stairs because we don't want to lose you.

Throw Rugs

Stand on one end of the throw rug to keep it in place. Don't use back-and-forth motions. Always vacuum away from where you're standing, lift up the beater head at the end of a stroke, and start again to the right. (Move forward on a long rug and repeat the process, if necessary, until you reach the other end.) Then come back to the starting point, where you had been standing originally, and do that area from the other direction—again pushing away from you and lifting the vacuum head at the end of a push.

When finished, wrap the cord around the vacuum and the extension cord around the cord caddy.

How to Vacuum with the Little Vac

Unless the Little Vac gets a lot of use (hardwood floors, for example), use it without a 50-foot extension cord. The Little Vac has several attachments. The attachment you choose depends on whether it's being used to vacuum the kitchen floor, the hardwood floors, or furniture.

When vacuuming noncarpeted floors, point the vacuum exhaust away from the area you have yet to vacuum so you don't stir up dust. Also, pay special attention to areas where there are electrical cords on the floor. The cords trap a lot of dust and debris, so slow down and vacuum carefully.

When vacuuming furniture, follow The Clean Team rules: Start on the left side at the top and work your way down and to the right.

Chapter 7.
THE OVEN

How often you do this chore depends on how often you use the oven. It's a messy and overnight job.

The first thing to notice when contemplating cleaning the oven is whether it is a self-cleaning species. If it is, follow the manufacturer's directions, not ours, and be thankful.

As long as your oven interior is a smooth baked-enamel finish (95 percent chance), you will find this chore yucky but manageable. If you have an oven whose interior feels like fine sandpaper, you have a problem, since the oven cleaner is very difficult to remove after the cleaning process. Give up.

Spray your oven the night before you are going to clean it. You'll need oven cleaner and rubber gloves. Before spraying the oven, remove the racks, placing them on top of the stove *the same way you took them out* (so you don't waste time later trying to figure out which is the top and how they go back in). Also remove anything else that should be removed, such as heating coils that pull out or unplug. Even if your whole interior oven comes apart for removal and cleaning, leave it together and clean it our way instead.

Put old cleaning cloths, paper towels, or newspapers on the floor to catch any drips and overspray. Spray the interior of the oven and the door as well. Often, the racks don't need cleaning. Skip them whenever you can, as they are difficult and time-consuming. If you are *not* cleaning them, leave them on top of the stove until you are done with the oven. If you are cleaning the racks, replace them after you have sprayed the inside of the oven and *then* spray them too. Spray the oven thoroughly: A little too much is better than not enough. If you overdo it, however, oven cleaner will drip onto the floor and make even more of a mess. Avoid the interior light and thermostat when spraying. Be sure to spray the door but not the door edges.

If you are going to clean the broiler too (wow!), then spray it now also. Just spray the broiler tray itself. Don't spray the holder grooves or underneath the broiler. Those areas don't have the cooked-on stuff and can be cleaned with Red Juice and your green pad. (Faster and eminently less messy.)

Put the racks back in if you haven't already, close the door, put away the oven cleaner, and go to bed. Don't heat the oven. Sweet dreams, for tomorrow you'll be up to your elbows in gook.

Next day—if you are also doing the weekly cleaning of the kitchen—clean the oven before you start the regular cleaning sequence. *Don't heat the oven.* Set the trash can by the stove for now, and place a roll of paper towels or old, disposable rags (ones that are no longer good enough to use as regular cleaning cloths) next to it. Also, take the

cleaning

scraper from your apron and put it on the cloths in front of the stove. You'll be using it repeatedly, and your gloves will be covered with oven cleaner. This way you'll keep the oven cleaner off your apron.

Start by *putting on the gloves!* First clean the inside of the oven door with your green pad. Use your razor on the glass door. Wipe the oven cleaner from the door. Then spray the same area with Red Juice and wipe it clean and dry. Clean the racks next, starting with the highest one. Use the green pad. Pull it out into the locked position to make cleaning easier. As you finish a rack, pull it out and set it in the sink. Rinse well with tap water. Be careful not to scratch the sink. (Use a cloth or two to put under the edges of the rack when rinsing.) After all the oven cleaner is removed, just let the racks drain and dry in the sink while you return to clean the next one down. As you clean them, pay special attention to the leading edges (the ones that you see when the rack is in the oven).

After the racks, clean the inside of the oven starting with the inside top. Systematically agitate with your green ʹpad over the entire top of the oven until all the baked-on residue is loose. But don't remove it yet. Move on to the right side, then the rear, and then the left side before you finish with the bottom. On areas where there are baked-on "lumps" (usually the bottom only), use your scraper first (remember, it's on the floor in front of the oven). The idea is to knock off most of what you're removing with the scraper first and then get what little remains with the green pad. Saves a lot of time.

Here the concept of "seeing through" the mess of what you're cleaning has particular meaning. Even if the oven were clean, you couldn't see through the oven cleaner. And unless you're much more compulsive than we are, your oven is not clean. You can quickly learn the difference between how your green pad feels when the oven surface is clean and how it feels on a dirty surface that needs additional scrubbing.

This "see-through" process is also especially important here because removing the oven cleaner is a big chore. If you've missed crud and have to respray and reclean, you may be tempted to give up cooking rather than go through it again.

Even after you've used the scraper to remove lumps, be prepared to grab for it quickly when you encounter something that your green pad doesn't easily remove.

As you may well have noticed, your green pad became a slimy, gooey, even yucky mess about half a second after you started this delightful chore. Resist the impulse to go to the sink and rinse the pad out. It will return to a slimy mess half a second after you return. It actually works just as well dirty for a long time. And, of course, the whole procedure is much faster if you don't make several trips to the sink to rinse.

When the pad is full of gunk and oven cleaner, it is harder to hold because it gets slippery. Try to overcome this by folding the pad in half or gripping it differently or squeezing it out onto the oven bottom—

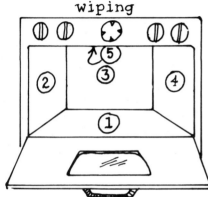

wiping

anything to avoid having to rinse it. When you just can't grip it any longer, go rinse it. Also if the oven is very dirty (especially when you're cleaning the bottom), your pad will lose its effectiveness when it gets thoroughly clogged with debris. When that happens, it's also time to go rinse. (Sounds like something your dentist would say.)

After you have gone over the entire oven this way, rinse out the green pad and scraper and put them in your apron. Start wiping the inside of the oven using paper towels or old rags. Wipe it out just the reverse of the way you just scrubbed it. Start with the bottom, then the left side, the rear, the right side, and finally the top. Wipe the entire oven out once, rather thoroughly—discarding the towels or rags into the trash can next to you. Now spray the entire inside of the oven with Red Juice and wipe clean and dry to get rid of any residual oven cleaner.

If the broiler was previously sprayed, now is the time to finish it. (Don't you really want to do this some other day?) Clean it in the sink with your green pad. Use your scraper if necessary . . . and it usually is. Protect the sink by putting cloths under the broiler. Rinse it clean, wipe it, and replace it.

Fold up the cloths (or paper towels), pick up the newspapers and discard into the trash, take a deep breath, and start cleaning the kitchen. It's a good idea to turn the oven to 400° for fifteen minutes while you start cleaning the kitchen. This cooks any oven cleaner you may have missed to a nice visible white powder that you can easily see to remove after the oven cools off. Also, if the oven is going to stink or smoke a bit, it's a good idea to get that little episode over with now instead of when you have company over for dinner.

You have cleaned an oven! Amazing how much better it looks—and you get all the credit! You may be tempted to go outside and stop strangers to bring them in and show them your clean oven. Resist: they may track in dirt.

Chapter 8.

THE REFRIGERATOR

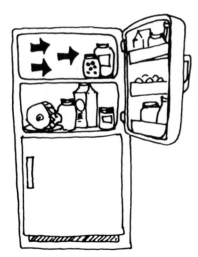

This is not weekly cleaning. However, if you are going to clean the refrigerator when you do your regular cleaning of the kitchen, do it first—before anything else. If the freezer is to be cleaned, it should have been turned off earlier so that it is defrosted and ready to clean. You can help yourself further with this chore by choosing a time to clean it when it's as empty of food as it gets (according to your weekly shopping schedule). Also, before starting, throw out anything that deserves it.

The freezer is easy to clean once the ice is loose. Put any loose ice and ice-cube trays in the sink and proceed to clean. If possible, don't remove anything else. Rather, move items toward the right, spray the left with Red Juice, and wipe. (If a little Red Juice gets on the frozen-food containers, it won't hurt a thing.) Now move items from the right to the left and repeat. You may have to do that in three moves or more. If the freezer is completely full, remove only as much as you have to. When you move items to make room for cleaning, move them onto the top shelf of the refrigerator.

Inside the refrigerator itself, start with the top shelf. These interior shelves don't usually need to be emptied. Items on the shelves should not be removed—just moved to the right. Then clean the racks with Red Juice and white pad, followed by a cleaning cloth to wipe dry. If the shelves are too full to move things to the side, then remove only enough so you can move the rest from side to side. When you remove items from a shelf, set them on a convenient countertop or on the floor just in front of the refrigerator in the order they were removed. After cleaning, replace the items in reverse order.

Do the next lower shelf and the next until you are finished. Drawers and bins should be removed from the refrigerator because you need to clean them inside and out. Don't forget that nasty area under the bottom drawers. Crud and water both accumulate here.

Generally you can clean the door shelves by removing a few items, cleaning that space, and then sliding over a few more things and cleaning under them, etc. Pick up and wipe the bottom of each item as you put it back so it doesn't leave a spot on the clean surface.

When you are finished with the inside of the refrigerator, don't clean the outside yet. Go back and start to clean the kitchen as you normally would. If you are working as part of a team, it often makes sense to have another team member do the inside of the refrigerator as you begin to clean the rest of the kitchen. The reason is that the kitchen can turn into the longest job, and you want the team to finish at the same time. (See Chapter 9.)

Chapter 9.
TEAM CLEANING

Goal

You may be lucky enough to have one or two others to work with. If so, someone needs to delegate the tasks and have a good overall view of the work as it progresses. That person is the Team Leader. The primary responsibility of the Team Leader is to see that all team members finish cleaning at the exact same time.

Finally, Some Decisions to Make

To finish together requires some decision making on your part. Like, where do you start cleaning so you'll finish together? When the Bathroom Person finishes his/her primary job, what's next? The same for the Kitchen Person.

The Longest Job

The key to finishing together is to identify the longest job and get it started at the right time. The longest job is the one that takes the longest time *and* that no one can help with. This is often the vacuuming.

When this longest job should be started is crucial. Get the longest job started early so it isn't still going on when the rest of the team is finished.

The graph on page 108 shows time wasted by starting the longest job (vacuuming) at the wrong time. The Bathroom Person ended up vacuuming while the other two stood idle. If the Duster had dusted only ten minutes, started the vacuuming, and then finished dusting, the whole team would have finished together. (See page 109.) They also would finish the entire housecleaning eighteen minutes faster apiece—that's nearly one full hour less total cleaning time per week!

The First Time

The first time you clean your home, you should start dusting in the living room. If you later find you're unable to avoid having the team end up in the same room toward the end of the cleaning job, then change your starting point to the master bedroom.

When the Other Team Members Finish Their First Job

As Team Leader, you should ask *whoever* finished first (usually the Bathroom Person) to start vacuuming in the rooms you have already dusted. He or she should start where you did and follow your same path.

When the Kitchen Person finishes, have him or her make the beds with you (assuming you make beds when you clean). *Don't* make a bed alone since two people can make a bed four times faster than one person. Then have the Kitchen Person start vacuuming the hardwood floors (using the Little Vac), also starting in the living room and following your same path through the house. The Kitchen Person can also use the Little Vac on any furniture as signaled by you. Next, he or she gathers up the trash by going from room to room and emptying smaller containers into the largest one so only one trip outside to the garbage can is made.

Important Points: Back to Basics

We hope all this doesn't sound difficult, because doing it is very easy:

1. If the longest job isn't finished when the rest of the jobs are, then start the longest job sooner the next time you clean.

2. If you all end up in the same room at the end, then dust that room sooner or vacuum it sooner or empty the trash from it sooner.

3. If the dusting job is taking too long, then have a second team member do some of the dusting.

4. If you aren't finishing together even after getting the longest job started earlier, save all the short jobs for last—emptying trash, making bed(s), putting throw rugs back in place, finishing touches, and checking each other's work (nicely, nicely).

5. If you still have problems finishing together, sit down and talk about it. Don't feel that just because you're Team Leader you are alone in a boat adrift. Try suggestions that come from the other team members.

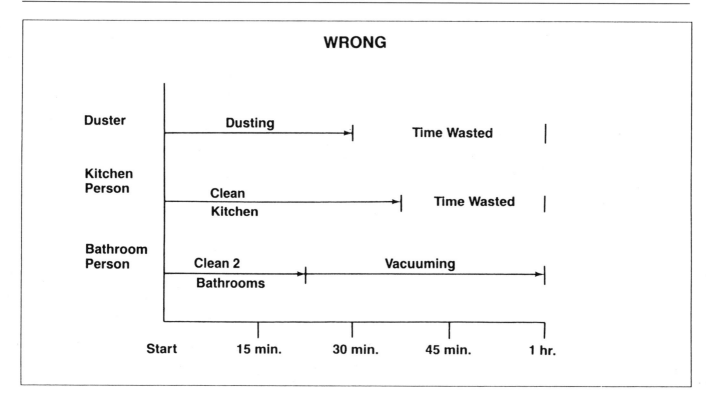

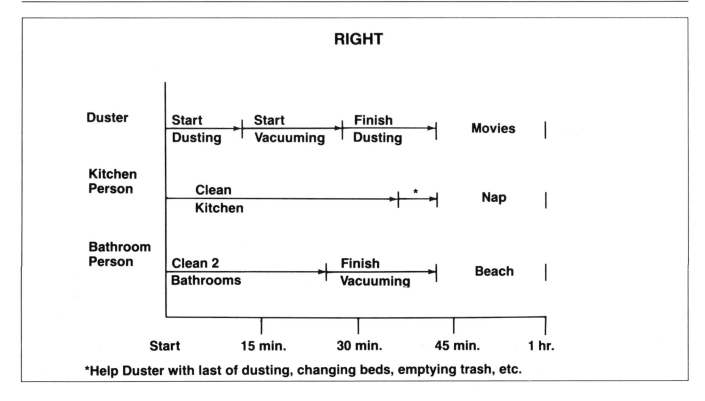

RIGHT

Duster	Start Dusting — Start Vacuuming — Finish Dusting — Movies
Kitchen Person	Clean Kitchen — * — Nap
Bathroom Person	Clean 2 Bathrooms — Finish Vacuuming — Beach

Start   15 min.   30 min.   45 min.   1 hr.

*Help Duster with last of dusting, changing beds, emptying trash, etc.

Team Cleaning in a Team of Three or More

Most of what we've discussed in this chapter applies to a team of three. The jobs are a Kitchen Person, a Bathroom Person, and the Duster. Teams of four or more are so inefficient (unless you have a huge house) that you may want to rotate people off each time you clean.

Team Cleaning in a Team of Two

In a team of two, one person starts as the Bathroom Person and the other as the Kitchen Person. The Team Leader is the one who finishes the initial assignment first—normally the bathroom. The Team Leader then changes the bathroom tray into a duster tray and starts dusting. The Kitchen Person starts vacuuming with the Big Vac after finishing the kitchen. Make adjustments so that each time the two of you clean you come closer and closer to finishing at the same time. It is much simpler for two people to finish at the same time than three, since there are fewer possibilities for how to divide up the work.

Team Cleaning in a Team of One

This is the most efficient way possible. No decisions, no negotiations—just follow the Speed Cleaning method and you get faster every time you do it.

Recording Your Improvement

You might want to chart your weekly housecleaning times so you can see how dramatically your time improves. Use it to motivate the members of your team during this critical learning period. Post it where it is easily seen, reviewed, and ultimately admired.

Chapter 10.
AN ENCOURAGING WORD

Did you ever despair of learning to tie your shoe, ride a bike, or swim? Can you remember how difficult it was to do something that is now mindless in its simplicity?

Did you ever learn touch-typing? If you did, you know that it took you longer to use touch-typing than your old hunt-and-peck method when you were first learning. You had to break comfortable old (inefficient) habits and replace them with unfamiliar, uncomfortable, and new (but very efficient) habits.

Also, if you used your old hunt-and-peck method of typing all day long every day, you would never, ever get much faster than 30 words a minute—even with all that practice. However, if you practiced your new touch-type method daily, you would improve your speed constantly: 100 words per minute is not an unheard-of speed. That's more than three times faster than a method that once seemed just fine to you.

Housecleaning isn't going to go away, so practice. Practice and be fast, and then do something much more fun or satisfying with all the time you saved.

"I did it your way, except I didn't use the apron since it doesn't really help me that much."

Chapter 11.
OTHER TYPES OF CLEANING

More!?

For those of you who see all the time-savings available in the preceding chapters but feel that your particular cleaning problem is still ignored and still overwhelming, you may be right.

Cleaning Categories

There are three types of household cleaning. One is weekly cleaning, which is the subject of this book. Unfortunately, there is also daily cleaning (clutter) and yearly ("spring") cleaning. Clearly, you are going to have trouble dealing with the weekly cleaning if no one is doing the daily cleaning.

Daily Cleaning (Clutter)

Daily cleaning is putting things in their place—day in and day out. Dirty dishes from the table (or TV room) into the dishwasher. Coats on their hangers. Dirty clothes into the hamper. The trash set out. The toys put away. Our third book will detail our system for clutter control and household organization. It will provide step-by-step relief if your household seems out of control at times (or in control only fleetingly). In the meantime, here are a few suggestions.

The best solution for reducing clutter is to handle each item once so it never gets a chance to become clutter. Put it away. Takes about two seconds. Try it. If that doesn't work you have too much stuff. Add a room, buy more furniture, or have a garage sale.

It may help to have designated "clutter areas." Once you have designated clutter areas, it's okay to throw things into them. Examples may be the corner next to the front door, one section of the kitchen counter, or the bedroom floor near the closet. After you get in the habit of putting things away in these areas, slowly reduce their size and then finally eliminate them.

Also, as promised in the introduction, once you start regular cleaning, these daily jobs will take care of themselves as a sense of pride in a clean home encourages everyone in the household to keep the home civilized between cleanings.

Yearly (Spring) Cleaning

Stripping wax from floors. Washing ceilings and walls. Or washing (heaven forbid) the windows. All those things that may need your cleaning attention once or twice a year. Happily, those chores have been addressed in our second book on cleaning, *SPRING CLEANING* (Dell, 1989).

Good luck with Speed Cleaning! May it change your life.

Chapter 12.
OUTSIDE CLEANING SERVICES

We've spent much of this book explaining our method for cleaning your home quickly. But what if you don't want to clean it at all? Hiring someone else to do the cleaning for you is appealing, but it also introduces a new list of issues, questions, and, well, problems.

There are three basic types of services, although their methods may vary considerably.

1. The Wonderful, Old-Fashioned Cleaning Lady

Some families are lucky enough to employ a cherished housecleaner who has been cleaning for them for years and is considered a part of the family. Unfortunately, as this group of housecleaners retires it seems there is no new generation coming along to replace them. Perhaps the number of people who view residential cleaning as a permanent career is dwindling. Maybe it just seems that way because there has been such an increased demand for cleaning services as millions of women have entered the work force.

2. Temporary Cleaning Persons

The demand is being filled by more people who are cleaning either temporarily or as a perceived last choice. There appears to be a disproportionate number of immigrants in this group who do not opt for more traditional employment because language difficulties or lack of legal status in the U.S. prevents them from obtaining other careers.

Even when someone comes along with an aptitude for and interest in cleaning, it may still be difficult to be a good cleaner because formal training is virtually nonexistent. Also, language barriers are real, and cultural differences can lead to interpretations of "cleaning" in ways you didn't anticipate, such as reorganizing your closets and drawers instead of actually cleaning the kitchen or bathroom.

Another component of this group that cleans on a transitory basis includes students, aspiring actors, dancers, artists, writers, and others who are cleaning until they get their diploma or big break, or until their ship comes in. But all these marvelously human situations are fluid, and as their fortunes rise or fall, you may lose your housecleaner.

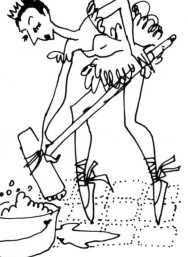

3. Cleaning Companies

In this case, a professional cleaning company hires, trains (ideally), and manages the housecleaner. If the housecleaner quits or is ill, it's up to the company to find a replacement. Some companies send individuals; others send teams.

The quality and reliability of these companies varies enormously but is generally improving as more people appreciate the opportunities available in this expanding industry. As more companies enter the cleaning field, they increase competition, which tends to improve service—in important areas such as cleaner training, customer relations, and reliability.

You might find the perfect cleaner in any of these groups, but before you even begin to look, there is a very important question that you must investigate. For whom does your housecleaner work? You or herself or himself? Once you've answered this question, you may know exactly in which of the above groups you want to look for a housecleaner. And if you already have a housecleaner, you may be inclined to make some changes once you've considered this same question.

For Whom Does Your Housecleaner Work?

This question has more practical importance than you may have imagined, because the answer to it may determine whether you are personally liable for back taxes and penalties when your house-cleaners (former and current) reach retirement and apply for Social Security benefits. In many cases, if their Social Security accounts are deficient, the IRS has been regularly ruling that their Social Security payments should have been paid by the people whose homes they cleaned. The IRS is ruling that the housecleaners were actually employees of the person whose house they were cleaning. That means you, gentle reader, and having an employee has a whole new set of rules.

If you hire a cleaning company that pays or withholds the necessary taxes and keeps the records that are required of businesses by the IRS, you shouldn't have much to worry about. Likewise, if you find your cleaner through an agency, the cleaner is generally not your employee if the agency is responsible for who does the work and how it is done. But if you find a cleaner through an agency or association that merely provides a list of housecleaners and does not regulate the hours of work, collect the pay, or set the standards and methods of work, the cleaner may very well be your employee. Likewise, if you hire an individual on the basis of a referral from a friend or neighbor, it's very possible that the cleaner is your employee.

Employee Versus Independent Contractor (Non-Employee)

There are good (or at least practical) reasons to prefer that your housecleaner *not* be your employee: It's less complicated and less costly. When someone is your household employee, you must collect, report, and match Social Security taxes, and sometimes pay federal unemployment taxes. Worker's compensation coverage must be provided for also.

Obviously it's much easier for you to call the housecleaner a non-employee or self-employed person. The proper term in this case is an independent contractor. If your housecleaner is an independent contractor, you do *not* have to withhold or pay any payroll taxes or file any employment reports or forms. All those things are the responsibility of the housecleaner—not you.

How Do You Tell the Difference Between an Independent Contractor and an Employee?

Ah! There's the rub. A typical example of an independent contractor is a lawyer hired to write a will. Although you are paying the lawyer, you don't have much control over his or her work—for example, how to write the will or what specific hours to work. And as long as the lawyer is doing the job properly, it won't be simple for you to dismiss him or her until the job is completed. For the IRS, control over the work of another person is probably the most important single distinction between an independent contractor and an employee.

In the case of housecleaning, if a worker performs services that are subject to your will and control—in terms of both what must be done and how it must be done—then that worker is your employee. It doesn't matter if you actually exercise this control as long as you have the legal right to control both the method and result of the cleaning services. Nor does it matter if you call the housecleaner an independent contractor. Nor does it matter if the housecleaner works full-time or part-time.

A few characteristics of an *employer* of a housecleaner are that the employer:

- has the right to discharge the cleaner
- supplies the cleaner with tools and a place to work
- directs the cleaner's work by means of instructions
- sets the hours or day of work
- or pays by the hour or day, not the job.

A ruling in any one of these traits may mean that your cleaner is an employee of yours. (For a list of all twenty factors the IRS takes into consideration, see IRS Publication 937—"Business Reporting.")

If you treat an employee as an independent contractor and you shouldn't have, it's possible that you'll get a bill for all of your housecleaner's Social Security taxes plus a fine of 100 percent!

Keeping a Secret

So, you ask, who cares about all this? You have no problems, right? You like your housekeeper and he or she likes you, and your way of paying wages has been working out just fine. So far.

Problems can and do arise a few years down the line when your housecleaner reaches retirement age and wants to start collecting Social Security benefits. If no one has been paying into that Social Security account, the housecleaner has no basis for collecting benefits.

Of course, what happens next is a stimulating discussion between the housecleaner and the IRS representative: The housecleaner has spent the last twenty years cleaning houses, so where are the retirement benefits that she or he has worked so hard to collect? Let's assume the housecleaner had paid income taxes every year, as many do. But no one had ever paid into his or her Social Security account. Maybe nobody even thought about it. Well, one thing leads to another, and, after a few seconds of deliberation, the IRS determines that the housecleaner was a household employee all those years—not an independent contractor as you had supposed. All of a sudden, you may be looking at a sizable tax bill.

IRS Rulings on This Subject

To test these waters, I filed three sets of Form SS-8 with our local IRS public affairs officer. These forms are called "Information for Use in Determining whether a Worker Is an Employee for Federal Employment Taxes and Income Tax Withholding." Whew. The IRS officer let me fill out this form with hypothetical cases, and agreed to make hypothetical rulings based on my three examples:

1. I filled out the first form as if I were the housecleaner. I described myself as an individual cleaner who cleans five different homes during the week, is expected to be there on a certain day, and is paid by the hour. I follow a list if left by the homeowner; otherwise I do the "normal cleaning."

2. I filled out the second form as if I were the homeowner. The working conditions were the same as in Form 1. I said I hired him because—on a different day of the week—he works for a neighbor who raved about his work.

3. I filled out the third form in exactly the same way as Form 2, except I said I hired the cleaner after finding a mimeographed flyer under my car's windshield wiper. In the flyer, the business was identified as "Ruth's Cleaning" and a phone number was given.

The IRS ruled that the housecleaner in all three cases was a "household employee." They based their decision on the control factor alone.

The IRS felt the client directed the housecleaner's work. That was enough for them—even in the case where the flyer was left soliciting business.

What the IRS Calls Your Housecleaner

It appears that the IRS regularly rules against many people who hired housecleaners who they thought were independent contractors, ruling instead that they are in a special category called "household employees." Here's the IRS's definition of the term:

> A homeworker who works by the guidelines of the person for whom the work is done, with materials furnished by and returned to that person or to someone that person designates.

Unlike standard employees, you do *not* have to withhold income taxes on wages paid to a household employee for services performed in or around your private home (unless the employee asks you to and you agree to do so). But if you pay a household employee $50.00 or more during a calendar quarter, you must withhold the employee's share of Social Security tax (FICA) from his or her wages, and you must match that amount from your own funds. It doesn't matter whether wages are based on the hour, day, week, month, or year. The value of food, lodging, clothes, bus tokens, and other noncash items given to household employees is *not* subject to FICA tax.

The IRS Will Make a Ruling for You

Tax regulations are almost always open to interpretation, and the employment status of your housecleaner may still require clarification before you feel confident of how to proceed. You may request the IRS to make a ruling for your particular set of facts and circumstances by filling in Form SS-8—the same one I sent in with three fictitious examples. *However,* this is *not* confidential information. If the IRS rules against you, they may follow up on it to see if you made any necessary changes.

How to Comply: Federal Requirements

If it turns out that your housecleaner is your employee, it really isn't too time-consuming or complicated to comply with these tax requirements. We've listed below the basic steps and the IRS forms you'll need. The forms are available at IRS offices or by calling 1-800-424-FORM. For additional general information on the subject, also request Publications 926 and 937 and Circular E. We must make the disclaimer that we're not tax experts, so be sure to check with the IRS, your accountant, lawyer, guru, or some other source if you have questions.

The Forms You'll Need

1. Employer Identification Number (EIN). Form SS-4.
2. Record keeping. Publication 926, page 4.

3. Social Security Taxes (FICA). Form 942 and Form W-2 for you and Form W-4 for your housecleaner.

4. Federal Unemployment Tax (FUTA). Form 940 (or 940-EZ) and Employer's Annual Federal Unemployment (FUTA) Tax Return.

5. Advance Payment of Earned Income Credit. Notice 797, Form W-5, Form 942, and Form W-2.

How to Comply: State Requirements

So far, we've not mentioned any state requirements. Check with your accountant, or place a call to your state employment or labor department to check the requirements in your particular state.

In California, for example, all homeowner's or renter's insurance policies must provide coverage for any household employees in your home. If you don't have such a policy, you are responsible for providing worker's compensation insurance coverage for your employee. It's not that unusual for housecleaners to hurt themselves while cleaning a home. A slip on a wet floor, a fall from a ladder, or a back thrown out from changing the bed or vacuuming could be a financial disaster if you don't have insurance for the housecleaner.

We've assumed throughout this discussion that the housecleaners are citizens or have legal status to work in the USA as aliens. If not, it's illegal for you to hire them as your employees. If they are working for a company or are independent contractors, you have no responsibility to determine their legal status. In that case it's between them and the Immigration and Naturalization Service—not you.

Independent Contractors' Income Reporting Requirements

The good news is that unless the payments you make to the independent contractor/cleaner are a business expense (i.e., used in the course of *your* trade or business), you don't have to report any payments made to them. In other words, if your housecleaner is not your employee, you do not have to file any report or fill out any tax form of any kind. If the payments you make to your cleaner are a business expense to you, report payments greater than $600 on IRS Form 1099.

No matter what the employment status of your cleaner, you still have the same goal: to get the house cleaned on a regular basis without having to do it yourself and with *less* grief and bother than if you did it yourself. Seems easy enough. Naturally, it's not. So now let's turn our attention to the management skills necessary to get the most out of your cleaner or cleaning service.

Roadblocks to Your Goal: Problems with Housecleaners

Here are the problems I have heard most often in the twelve years I've been in this business. The housecleaner:

- doesn't come on the day or time scheduled
- doesn't understand English well enough

- rearranges the furniture and doesn't put things back in their place
- doesn't clean well enough
- doesn't know how to clean
- charges too much
- breaks things
- doesn't follow (or forgets) directions
- substitutes personnel too often
- doesn't accept responsibility for accidents
- won't do extra chores (windows!)
- is too much trouble to get ready for
- quits, and you have to start over again
- eats the cupboards bare
- steals things
- is too nosy.

If you're tired of trying to correct these problems, and if throwing good money at them is beginning to seem like more trouble than cleaning your house yourself, we've got some suggestions. We realize that we're often asking you to change instead of the cleaner. It's not a perfect world. And sure, there are plenty of housecleaners who should be fired or should be, perhaps, truck drivers instead. But if you're willing, you can learn techniques to stay in charge, to create a better work place, and to motivate your cleaner to get the job done the way you want it done. Basically, we suggest *managing* your housecleaner as you would anyone who works for you in the office or at home.

The Benefits of Managing

Honing your management skills can really pay off, because most housecleaners are ever so slightly less than perfect. That includes The Clean Team! But certain customers really know how consistently to get the very best we have to offer, despite our limitations. We've cleaned for some of these folks for years, with inevitable personnel changes on our teams. But these customers manage to get even the newer cleaners to perform as if they had been around for much longer, to work harder, to apply themselves more diligently, to agree to do extra tasks, to take pride in their work—and to do all this with a smile and a feeling that these clients are really special.

Naturally, this isn't just luck. These customers realize that their hiring options are extremely limited. They can hire only perfect housecleaners (quite difficult to do). Or they can hire and motivate someone with the potential to be a very good housecleaner.

Johnson and Blanchard said in *The One Minute Manager:* "Everyone is a potential winner."[1] Like the favorite clients I mentioned above, good managers promptly turn potential into hardworking reality. These clients are those "lucky" people who always seem to find a great cleaner or cleaning service (or contractor or dry cleaner or dentist). Exactly! They create that luck through good management.

Your Home as a Great Place to Work

Your home is the housecleaner's place of business. Is it a good place to work? The spirit or morale of your household is set by you. It's more than a matter of trying to get along with your housecleaner; the human relations between you and your housecleaner are grounded in job satisfaction and job performance. Friendliness without these other foundations inevitably results in poor morale. If you create a positive work environment in your home, your housecleaner will feel good about the work and will be free to do his or her best. People who feel good produce good results.

The best way to create good morale is to look for people's strengths. Peter Drucker, in *The Practice of Management*, says: "Nothing destroys the spirit of an organization faster than focusing on people's weaknesses rather than on their strengths, building on disabilities rather than abilities."[2]

Motivating

Your housecleaner is a resource. However, the housecleaner has absolute control over whether she or he works at all, so your house-cleaner as a resource has got to be motivated. Fear is not much of a motivator anymore. In a society able to provide subsistence to the unemployed, fear has lost much of its grip. Besides, firing people doesn't get the work done.

Motivating doesn't mean you have to be autocratic or hard-nosed. Positive motivation is usually far more successful than negative. But purely democratic, participative, supportive, or humanistic ideals alone aren't enough either. Money is important, but it's largely a negative incentive; being unhappy with pay is a powerful disincentive, but satisfaction with pay motivates only when other factors are working. A high wage won't keep people motivated if they hate every minute they spend at work, or if they are belittled, or if they feel exploited.

Here are six specific ways to motivate your housecleaner.

1. Start with yourself and set high standards:

- Remember that you're the boss. A good boss is supposed to be wise, fair, and decisive. In this setting these qualities are expected of you as the manager of this small enterprise—your home. Your housecleaner will find it hard to be motivated to excellence if the boss is disorganized, ill-prepared, disinterested, or inept.
- Have the house ready so the housecleaners can start upon arrival. If, for example, you have to pick up the house before they can do the cleaning, be sure it's done. Don't make them clean around any chaos.
- Have all the needed supplies on hand, plus a spare bag for the vacuum or a new one installed beforehand.
- Be sure your equipment is in good condition: no clogged vacuum wands, no empty spray bottles. Have a spare vacuum belt available, plus any tools and instructions needed.
- Be sure to have meaningful work to be done. Even if you have to take time to plan, don't have just "busy work" to be done.

2. Give housecleaners all the information necessary to be in control of their work and to be able to deliver a responsive performance. The housecleaner has to know what you want done, how you want it done, where things go, what not to touch, and so on. This is how job satisfaction starts. There's almost no better way to destroy morale than not letting someone know how to satisfy expectations. One can try hard but never have it turn out to be right or enough.

3. Let your housecleaners know how important their work is to your home and/or family as a whole. Tell them how their contributions improve your home life, reduce stress, afford you valuable extra time, etc. Allow them to see your household as if they were responsible, through their performance, for some of the success of your household.

4. Allow the housecleaners to participate in the planning of the job. They are more likely to feel responsible for the results if they helped plan the job itself. Don't detail them to death with what you want done, in what order, and how to do it. To be motivating and satisfying, work needs some element of challenge, skill, and judgment.

5. Establish and sustain rapport by leaving your housecleaners a note every time they visit; address them by name. Thank them for last week's extra work; explain that because the sink's a mess this week they can skip it; swear undying loyalty; tell them Aunt Bunny is coming and the spare room needs special attention; pass on a good joke; tell them there's a treat in the cookie jar. Try to keep your notes upbeat. And you'll get answers. This is a dialogue—and dialogue is critical to

managing and motivating. We have clients who look forward nearly as much to the weekly note as to the clean house.

Leave your note every single time—not just when you have extra requests or a reminder or a complaint. Consider how you'd feel if the only words you ever had from your employer or client were negative. A note with no special instructions—such as "nothing special today, just the usual great job"—is just as important as the ones that are chock-full of instructions. But when you do need to work out a problem, it will be much easier on you both if it's part of a regular weekly note.

6. Probably the most effective motivators of all are the simple expressions of thanks and appreciation for work well done: "Fantastic job!" "I could not have done that better myself, and you know how particular I am about my kitchen." "Thank you so much for working so hard on those horrible shower walls." "Thank you for all your efforts. You make our home and life so much more comfortable and pleasant."

Praise doesn't have to be lavish, but people do need to know their efforts are noticed and appreciated. A good manager knows this and never fails to act on it. Invariably, a simple "thanks" will guarantee an even better job done the next time. Especially don't forget to acknowledge the effort put into a special request or project.

Rewards and small considerations are great if they are sincere and appropriate. Cookies, holiday cards, or candy are all effective ways to express appreciation or thanks.

Management If Your Housecleaner Is NOT Your Employee

Management of a housecleaner (or a team) who works for a company is effectively the same as managing your own employee. Think of yourself as a midlevel manager. The difference is that you aren't directly in charge of the cleaners; you can correct their work only up to a certain point before you need to talk to their boss. This type of relationship limits your control. But it doesn't limit your using all your managing and motivating skills.

Proven Ways to Get the Most out of Your Housecleaner, Solve Problems, and in General Have Everything Go Swimmingly

1. Selecting a Cleaner or Cleaning Service

Of course, the best way to know whom to call is via a recommendation from a neighbor or relative or friend. If you were so lucky, you probably wouldn't be reading this.

Start with names from a friend, from a flyer in the mail, from the Yellow Pages, from an ad on the side of a bus, or from a billboard. Then call them up and interview them on the phone. Ask them to tell you what they clean and what they prefer to clean. For example, here in San Francisco there are cleaners who clean only empty homes or apartments, who clean only after fires or other insurance-related events, who clean only on a one-time basis, who clean only carpets, and so on.

Ask if they clean in your neighborhood.

Ask about their experience. How long have they been in business? Have they had any formal training?

They should be able to give you a reference. Give them a couple of days to check with one of their customers to get permission to give their name and telephone number to you. But don't necessarily give up on a particular individual or company if they don't have a reference. Some people are reluctant to give out their names and telephone numbers to strangers.

Also check with the Better Business Bureau. Poor cleaning services accumulate a negative file with the BBB rather quickly. Bear in mind that individual cleaners are less likely to have complaints filed against them with the BBB.

If you're looking for ongoing household cleaning, the service should make an appointment to see your home in order to give you an estimate. You may prefer that they just come and clean your home once so you can see if their work is any good. However, most companies really do need to know how much work there is before they can schedule you, and countless potential misunderstandings can be

avoided by having them see your home prior to cleaning it the first time. Read on.

2. Rates: By the Hour

It's more important how much work gets done per hour than what the hourly rate is. But many people still shop by comparing hourly rates. It's no bargain to pay $4.00 per hour for eight hours of work when someone else can finish the job in far less time at a higher rate—especially if the lower-paid worker is not very experienced, is a mediocre cleaner, or is unreliable.

If you have a housecleaner you like, it can be to your advantage to pay by the hour. Housecleaners will get faster and faster at cleaning your home as they do it over and over again. So after a few months, cleaning your home may only take them three hours instead of the five hours it originally took. For the same price, you can now have the housecleaner do some ironing, wash a few windows, polish some brass or silver, or do some other chore that wasn't originally included in the housecleaning.

3. What Should Be Done for a Fixed, Per-Visit Fee?

Many housecleaners or cleaning companies charge by the job instead of the hour, especially for ongoing cleaning. It might take them a little longer one time and a little shorter the next, but it averages out.

A fixed job price has many advantages: you know how much work will get done, you don't have to worry whether they work fast or slow, or take breaks on your time. All you have to consider is whether the price is fair and the house is clean.

It also gives housecleaners a chance to earn more money per hour by concentrating on being efficient. This is a real morale-booster because they can earn the same amount of money in fewer hours. Working more efficiently and smarter doesn't mean that the quality of work suffers. In fact, quite the opposite is commonly true because the work that is done is given full attention.

A fixed price assumes a job description: exactly what work is going to be done for the price. Generally, the job description is for "light housecleaning," which should include all the things you would normally clean once a week or every other week if you were doing the work yourself.

Cleaning tasks not included in the job description are yearly or "spring cleaning" chores, such as washing windows, stripping wax off floors, polishing silver, cleaning ovens, washing walls and ceilings, and cleaning carpets. Expect to pay extra for many of these chores.

A job description has to assume that the house is ready to be cleaned so the housecleaner can go right to work. People often joke that they have to clean up before the cleaners arrive. But what we're really talking about is picking up the house so the cleaners can get to the surfaces they are supposed to clean. Picking up is daily cleaning, and a good example is the kitchen. We can't clean the sink if it's full of dirty dishes. That doesn't mean that they can't be washed; it just means that if you want to include a *daily* cleaning job like the dishes, you'll need to discuss it and expect to pay for it.

4. Giving the Key to Your Home to a Stranger

Housecleaners usually will want to clean when you're at work. They need a reliable, fail-safe way to get into your home—usually a key.

There are a few alternatives to providing a key. A doorman, baby-sitter, neighbor, or landlord are all fine as long as they never leave the house. Our exhaustive experiments have shown that, without fail, the moment your neighbor runs to the store for a quart of milk The Clean Team will arrive. It is surprisingly difficult to arrange fail-safe access via a third party.

Some clients attempt to solve their security fears by scheduling the housecleaners to clean when the clients have a day off. This is a great way to ruin an otherwise perfectly good day. It is very frustrating to have plans for your day off and then find yourself waiting for a housecleaner who has been delayed. Even if the housecleaner does arrive on time, you may quickly discover that you don't appreciate having someone underfoot.

Absolutely don't leave the key under the door mat! Not only do burglars know about this favorite hiding place, but if there ever were a burglary at your home, how would you know who did it? At least if the housecleaner or cleaning company has a key and something is missing, you have a good chance to collect from a reputable housecleaner or company.

Some cleaning companies provide the client with a lockbox and a key to open it. The client puts a key to the house into the lockbox, which is usually hung on the outside doorknob. The housecleaner also has a key to the lockbox and uses it to retrieve the house key, which is replaced upon leaving. We're not sure how much this improves security. If the housecleaners were dishonest, they could still go copy the keys and replace the originals in the lockbox without the client's knowledge.

Needless to say, it's scary to hand over a key, but there seem to be few other options that are any safer and yet still accomplish the purpose. Some people with deadbolts offer only the doorknob key; we have yet to find a client who does not then forget to leave the deadbolt unlocked. In addition, the house is left less secure that day with just the one lock in place, whether we get in to clean or not.

When The Clean Team asks clients to mail us a key, we advise them to take one precaution: not to put their return address either inside or outside the envelope. We tell them to identify the key by name or initials only. We watch for it and call them when it arrives. Once we get the key, we number it and file it in a safe with no reference to name or address. Even if a team should lose a whole ring of keys, they would still be useless to whoever found them.

5. Security Alarms

Teach the housecleaners how to arm and disarm the house's security system. There are two problems if you leave it disarmed on the day the cleaning service comes. First, of course, your home isn't as secure as it would be if the alarm were on all day. And second, you have to remember to disarm it. What you really have to do is to remember *not* to do something that you usually do—which is surprisingly difficult. Most alarm systems have special codes that are designed to be used by people who need occasional access to your home. Consider using that feature instead of deactivating your whole alarm system.

6. What about Insurance?

This is a tough one. Most services can and should have a bond to cover employee theft, usually for a fixed dollar amount. The problem with bonds is that most require a conviction before the bonding company will pay a claim, and the evidence is likely to be circumstantial: You didn't see anyone take it, and there's no physical evidence that the housecleaner did it instead of a neighbor or a burglar.

It would also be nice if the cleaning company had liability insurance to provide for relief in case a Ming vase is broken or, heaven forbid, the housecleaner somehow manages to set your house on fire. Many cleaning companies don't have liability insurance to cover these disasters. We carried it at The Clean Team for the first five or six years we were in business. Each year our rate spiraled higher and higher even though we never had a claim. We finally canceled it the year that the annual premium would have nearly equaled our total net pay.

There is a solution. Many homeowner's policies will cover damage done in your home by household workers. Call your insurance agent and ask.

7. Scheduling, Cancellations, and Lateness

From what we hear, the most common complaint about cleaners is that they don't show up on their appointed day. You'd better talk to prospective housecleaners about this one. They will say they're reliable. But ask them what happens if they don't show up on the appointed day. Will they guarantee one free cleaning as a recourse?

This same problem, as viewed by your housecleaner, arises when you cancel cleaning visits. If you call and cancel the cleaning on short notice, you have taken one giant step toward ruining your relationship with your housecleaner.

If a genuine emergency does arise, at least try to reschedule the cleaning for the next day or two. Housecleaners will appreciate your trying to protect their income by rescheduling rather than skipping a visit entirely. We have clients that use us even when they're on vacation: They can ask us to substitute some chores for the regular weekly

cleaning—like washing windows or stripping floors—and we can also help keep the plants alive. This kind of loyalty shown to one of our teams by a client seems to motivate that team all year long.

Lateness is usually a problem only if you've been unable to find a way to arrange access for your cleaners. (They have no house keys, in other words.)

8. Breakage!

The most common "breach of security" in homes with housecleaners is not theft—it's breakage. Who pays for it if the housecleaner breaks something? Ask. Your prospective housecleaner or cleaning service should have a policy for taking care of such events.

Our policy is that if we break something, we'll pay for it up to $500. Above this amount the client needs to depend on homeowner's insurance. There are two exceptions. If the item was already broken, we don't want to be held responsible, and we would like the client to tell us about it before we even touch it. (Make sure to tell new cleaners about your home's booby traps. Like that lamp shade that falls off a particular lamp if you look at it cross-eyed. Everyone in your family knows it, but when the unsuspecting housecleaner turns on the lamp to be able to clean, the shade comes crashing down. Even worse, it lands on several other items that weren't broken before, but they certainly are now.)

The second exception is when we clean something, using standard accepted methods ("due diligence"), and it still breaks. For example, we dust a picture hanging on the wall with a feather duster just as we've done many times before. This time, however, it crashes to the floor, which breaks it and our nerves. If the client hangs the picture with a thumbtack, the client pays for this type of damage.

Tell the housecleaner about any items in your home that are so valuable to you that if anyone ever breaks them, it had better be you. Many items are valuable for strictly personal reasons that no one could ever guess. Tell your cleaner not even to touch them—that they're very precious to you and you will clean them yourself. You can use the same rationale to protect other frail objects, heirlooms, artwork, or expensive stereos. Why give trouble an engraved invitation? It will usually invite itself in anyway.

Federal laws on working conditions say that if your housecleaner is your employee, you may not charge him or her for breakage unless you can prove gross negligence or a willful or dishonest act. The law is specifically written so that the burden of proof is squarely on the employer.

9. Complaints: Satisfaction Guaranteed?

Some people think there is exactly one way to clean a house—their way. If you have tendencies in this direction, try not to complain about your housecleaners' methods when their actual results are acceptable.

But if the end result isn't satisfactory, any housecleaner or cleaning service should have some policy for handling complaints and ensuring your satisfaction. When you inquire, have strong doubts about hiring the services of someone whose reply is something like, "Oh, there's nothing to worry about. We never have complaints." Really?

Your housecleaner or cleaning service should handle your complaints the same way any other well-run business does. You should receive an apology and an offer to make it right. The Clean Team offers to come back the next day to correct any oversight. If customers don't want us to do that, they may reduce the charge for the next cleaning by an amount they feel is appropriate. Finally, if the customers are so upset that they don't want us to return, we offer a full refund.

If you're generally satisfied with your housecleaner but suspect he or she has overlooked something, you'll find you get better results if you fully consider your complaints. Before you accuse, stop and think. Maybe the floor that doesn't seem clean was an ungodly mess from your party the night before. Maybe the housecleaner cleaned it, but missed a spot or two. Accusing conscientious housecleaners of skipping something is tantamount to calling them a liar. If you sincerely think a complaint is justified, ask before you accuse.

But don't be afraid to mention something that needs more attention or that's not quite up to your standards or expectations. This can be done in a positive and beneficial way, if you'll just give your words some prior thought. The antidote to anger is gentleness. If your complaint is presented in an appreciative and supportive manner—"We're working on this together"—it will generally be quickly solved.

It's a good idea to state your complaint right away. If you wait until it's happened over and over, you'll weaken your own credibility. Would you like be told you'd make a mistake over and over? Wouldn't you rather be told the first time so you could correct it right away?

And try to balance a request for more or better effort with a few kind words about something else that is being well done. It's easy to begin to take consistent hard work for granted.

Here are some notes from one of our clients who does a good job of getting the very best from us. (She's actually complaining, but it's just about painless, and it gets the job done.)

"Maybe it's just that time of year, but there seems to be more dust around than usual. Would you give it your critical and special touch this week?"

"I've moved a few pieces of furniture out from the walls to make it easier for you to get into those hard-to-reach corners that seem to love dirt and grime."

"We would appreciate it so much if you could give some thought or ideas on how to remove the grease build-up around the top of the stove and the stove pipe. What do you think? Should we try a better cleaning agent? Do you have a preferred favorite? As always, thank you for your help."

Just as you need to be able to complain, so should the housecleaners. You will make giant strides in positive motivation if you make it clear that you are open to feedback also. Keep communication open.

10. Leaving Cookies and Milk:
Is the Cleaner Welcome to Raid the Fridge?

If you provide your cleaner with lunch, the cleaner should eat what you offer. Whether or not you should offer lunch is an easy problem to solve. Just ask. The housecleaner's expectation will be made very clear to you. Until you discuss it or make an offer in one of your notes, the housecleaner should not raid the fridge. Offering something refreshing, a soft drink, for example, may enhance motivation, is appreciated, and isn't very expensive. And we've gotten notes from dieting customers who have a supply of cookies or cake on hand that is tempting them too much: "*Please* eat *all* the cookies."

Also, consider whether the cleaner is welcome to turn on the TV, stereo, VCR, or the like. It is somewhat startling to turn on the stereo (which you had left tuned to the easy-listening station) and be blasted halfway across the room by acid rock. But most people do enjoy listening to music while they work. If it's all right with you, but not all right with your spouse, make some decision on the subject and discuss it with the housecleaner. (The discussion beforehand with your spouse is important. It's demoralizing to the housecleaner to get chewed out by the husband for something the wife explicitly said was okay.)

11. Who Supplies the Cleaning Products and Equipment?

The Clean Team supplies everything—mops, polish, cleaning cloths, cleansers, two vacuums, everything. We don't want to waste time looking for your supplies. As long as you don't object to particular supplies, it saves you time and money if the cleaners bring their own supplies. Careful: Two cleaning services may charge about the same, but one brings its own supplies and the other expects you to buy them. That's really a big difference in effective cost.

12. They Can't Clean Every House on Friday

The cleaning service probably works Monday through Friday. This means they need to clean about 20 percent of their accounts each day and can't clean everyone's house on Friday. In a city the size of San Francisco, we can't afford to clean for someone on a certain day unless we're already in the neighborhood. To drive across town to clean one house would often take longer than the housecleaning itself. Besides, if the housecleaners come soon after a weekend instead of just before it, they can clean up after the mess made over the weekend, you'll enjoy your clean house for a much longer period of time, and you'll end up with more for your money.

13. Other Types of Security

There are ways security can be breached that go beyond leaving keys.

I remember a client, a doctor, who had brought home some original patient files, test results, and X rays to study at home. These items weren't supposed to have left the hospital. She smuggled them home in a paper bag. After she was finished with them, she replaced them in the paper bag and set the bag on top of the small wastebasket next to a desk. Naturally, we threw them away! And as fate would have it, the garbage was picked up before the doctor got home.

We've thrown away rings that had been mixed in with the cigarette butts left in an ashtray. We've heard of a cleaner who diligently stacked and straightened all the papers on an accountant's desk just as she did every time she cleaned. Problem was, on that particular week the papers were tax records and expense receipts for several people. Once they were neatly stacked, it was almost impossible to figure out what belonged to whom.

Even when you completely trust your housecleaner, don't leave things lying about out of place. Besides the obvious temptation, you're asking for other headaches. The housecleaner might drop a ring left on the kitchen counter into a cleaning apron pocket, intending to put the ring on the bedroom dresser where it belongs. By the time he or she gets to the dresser, the cleaner has forgotten all about it and then tossed all the "trash" from the apron at the end of the day. An honest housecleaner, but you're missing a ring.

14. Protect Your Household's Privacy

Like any normal household, you undoubtedly have a secret or two that you hope and pray absolutely no one will discover. English author W. Somerset Maugham (1874–1965) has said, "There is hardly anyone whose sexual life, if it were broadcast, would not fill the world at large with surprise and horror." Human nature being what it is, you might want to be sure that certain items are returned to the back of the dresser drawer, for example. Or that certain papers (especially financial ones) are replaced in the locked desk drawer. Certain pictures or videos should be put away. You get the idea.

15. Special Instructions

Let's say you know that the instant your housecleaner turns on the vacuum cleaner, your cat will head straight for the hall closet and will stay hidden there long after the vacuuming is finished. So tape a note to the closet door saying *"DO NOT CLOSE."* Your house is not the only one your housecleaners work in. Especially on the first few visits, don't rely on their memory of everything you mentioned the first time you met. We all forget instructions occasionally, and most of us appreciate friendly reminders and warnings.

Other changes in your household from week to week may have little

to do with security, but if handled incorrectly can make you feel as if *something* has been breached. A new puppy in your home or a school project in the middle of the living room are examples. If you were doing the cleaning, you would certainly know what to do about each of them. The housecleaners may not. Don't leave it to chance. Tell them.

16. Tipping

Since the housecleaner performs a personal service (like a haircutter, waiter, or cab driver), tipping is appropriate when deserved. A few customers leave a small tip each visit or for a special project or effort, but most leave something at Christmas. Some leave gifts like food or wine instead of cash. But a gift of cash—and not a check—is preferred by most housecleaners. One guideline is to leave an amount equivalent to one month's cleaning charges. This amount would be split if more than one person does the cleaning.

17. Training

Training is a very touchy subject when it comes to housecleaners, particularly if they're in business for themselves and are not your employees. They already know how to clean and may not be the least bit interested in learning how to clean any differently than they now do—especially any faster if they are working by the hour.

However, many cleaning services are perfectly willing to consider ideas from other experts. They want to know about anything that may save them time, techniques that may save wasted energy, or products that may save their health. Naturally, we believe that suggesting or giving them this book and outfitting them with an apron and some cleaning tools are excellent ideas.

If the person cleaning for you is your employee, you can train him or her any way you like. *SPEED CLEANING* is custom-made for your situation. Your employee will be a better cleaner and will have more time available to do other things. Use our book as a training manual, and write or call us if you would like to order any of the supplies we use. If you or your housecleaner has a question, call or write. We're happy to help in any way we can.

18. Language Problems

It's most difficult to communicate if you and your housecleaner speak different languages. Sometimes translation services are available through the agency that sent the cleaner or through a few civic or religious organizations. But there aren't enough of them and they aren't uniformly available.

We've added a Spanish-language summary to this book that will be helpful if Spanish is the foreign language involved. We have other training in development in different mediums (for example, on videotape). You may call us at (415) 621-8444 for more information if these training tools would be helpful.

NOTES

1. Kenneth Blanchard and Spencer Johnson, *The One Minute Manager* (New York: Berkley Books, 1982).
2. Peter F. Drucker, *The Practice of Management* (New York: Harper & Row, 1954).

Chapter 13.

ENVIRONMENTAL IMPACTS OF HOUSEHOLD CLEANERS

As most of us learned long ago, dirt and grime don't just roll over and give up when they see us coming. So consumers have often turned to powerful cleaning agents to help the cause. These agents can have potentially harmful consequences on the environment long after they're washed down the drain.

This is a time of transition—when many formerly cholesterol-happy cooks are turning to tofu. Likewise for cleaners' technology—people are seeking ways to turn from hazardous cleaning agents to relatively benign ones. But this transition in technologies has only just begun. Accordingly, many recommendations in publications on the environment turn out to be personal beliefs or preferences that are not backed up with scientific data. We've sifted through these recommendations and integrated them with our own experience, and we list below our review of the products we use in terms of their probable environmental impacts. We have also listed alternatives in case you have other preferences.

It is important to distinguish between hazards to individual health and hazards to the environment. The two are often inextricably entwined, but not always. For example, a product can be an irritant to an individual but can biodegrade quickly and thoroughly enough to pose little environmental hazard. On the other hand, a product may not be much of a personal irritant but may promote excessive growth of algae downstream in the waste cycle. By and large, when there's a lack of environmental data, some publications shift to descriptions of personal hazard. Until the environmental data are in, one way of reasoning is that if a little of a product is personally hazardous, then a lot of it is likely to be environmentally hazardous too. That's not always the case, but it's often a good start.

Our own selection of the products we use (The Clean Team supplies our own products) was motivated by a strong desire to avoid products that caused health problems or irritation to ourselves. Our teams are exposed to five or more complete household cleanings every workday, so if there's a problem with a product it's readily apparent. None of the products we have recommended in this book, when used as described, have caused our teams health problems. Admittedly that is not an accurate index of their environmental impact, but we take it as a favorable sign.

Alternative formulas for brand-name cleaning products are being proposed by environmentalists as safer—both environmentally and personally. Some of these formulas are mixtures of several ingredients. Many environmentalists seem to believe that if one cleaner is good, then several mixed together ought to be that much better. But that's often not true. When you combine a second or third active ingredient, you can generate a chemical free-for-all, especially considering that there are so many trace compounds in ordinary tap water to begin with. In addition, mixtures of ingredients can work at cross purposes— such as mixing an acid and an alkali in the same formula. Unless a mixture of multiple ingredients has been thoroughly tested by someone with a competent background, stick with single-ingredient alternatives.

One of the most famous and dangerous combinations of household cleaners is chlorine bleach and ammonia, which produces potentially harmful chloramine fumes. But mixing chlorine bleach with other cleaning agents like acids—vinegar and phosphoric acid, for example—can liberate chlorine gas, which can be as toxic as chloramine.

Face Masks

By the way, you may be tempted to wear a face mask when working with cleaners to avoid exposure to fumes. But most cheap particle masks filter out only large dust particles—not vapors. To block vapors from cleaning agents you would need a cartridge-type or industrial-grade mask with an air supply (both of which require medical consultation before use if you are overweight, smoke, or have a heart condition). In most cases for household work, a mask seems unnecessary if you've provided the abundant ventilation that is called for in the directions for just about all cleaning products.

Rubber Gloves

Wearing rubber gloves, by contrast, is almost always a sensible idea when working with strong household cleaners. Unfortunately, many consumer varieties don't effectively resist strong cleaning agents. We use a very thick type that resists even formaldehyde. They're also 16 inches long, which helps a great deal to avoid those clammy dribbles down our arms and inside the glove when cleaning.

General Considerations

Before we consider individual products, let's review a few ideas about environmental impacts that apply to many cleaners. Often the easiest way to clean in an environmentally sound way is simply to reduce the amount of the product used: use one paper towel instead of three; apply a tablespoon of Comet rather than half a cup. And use durable tools instead of disposable gimmicks: brushes, not disposable swipes.

Several products require reasonable caution when disposing large amounts down the drain—notably chlorine bleach and ammonia. The

P trap under the sink is made of relatively thin metal, and undiluted chlorine bleach can eat right through it if given the chance. So keep the cold (not hot!) water running if you pour a quart or more of bleach down the drain. Actually, the toilet is the preferred means of disposing of reasonable amounts of cleaner, except for ammonia (see below). To comply with laws for disposal of significant quantities of bleach or other potentially hazardous substances, contact hazardous-waste authorities in your area for the recommended procedure.

For your personal protection, provide abundant ventilation when using any strong cleaner. For prolonged exposure to powerful fumes like those of ammonia, bleach, and pine-oil cleaners, knowledgeable sources recommend exhausting the fumes out the window with a fan. (Presumably you are prudent enough not to be situated between the window and the fumes.) Another way to avoid respiratory exposure is to use pump-spray products instead of aerosols. This applies especially around children.

Labels

Most of us believe we can get reasonable information from labels regarding environmental and personal hazard. But consumer labels are not required to disclose many, many potentially dangerous substances. Why? The Consumer Products Safety Commission (CPSC) has limited jurisdiction. They can require a listing of an ingredient on a consumer label only if the substance is defined as a hazardous substance by one specific law (the Federal Hazardous Substances Act). And they can ban an ingredient only if an adequate label cannot be written for that listed ingredient (e.g., if adequate first-aid instructions cannot be given on a label).

What is covered by this federal law? Only substances that pose an acute (immediate) hazard—not chronic (long-term) hazards. Swell. If it doesn't knock you over on the first whiff, you don't have to be informed about it (with one or two exceptions—like asbestos). What does this exclude? Oh, merely *carcinogens* (agents that causes cancer), *mutagens* (agents that cause genetic mutations), and *teratogens* (agents that cause birth defects)! And just because the Occupational Safety and Health Administration (OSHA) itself declares something to be a contaminant doesn't mean you have to be informed about it on the label of the product you'll be using in your home.

Such ingredients must be listed for industrial usage via something called a Material Safety Data Sheet (MSDS). You can request an MSDS for a retail product from the manufacturer, who will usually voluntarily comply.

There's little point in jumping all over the CPSC, because their jurisdiction is limited by law. Their budget hasn't increased since 1973, and it's an amount that the Pentagon probably spends in five minutes. The people to contact live in the White House and work in the House and Senate. Tell them consumers need fuller disclosure on consumer labels so we can make up our own minds about what we're introducing into our own homes and bodies. Thank you.

Red Juice

We started looking for a nonirritating general-purpose cleaner within a few days of starting The Clean Team. The grocery-shelf cleaners made most of us cough, especially in confined spaces. We ended our search with a unique product from Oregon.

It's no accident that our Clean Team Red Juice is environmentally safe. It was designed to be that way. Dirt clings to surfaces like a stretched elastic membrane. Without getting into too much chemistry, Red Juice is basically a unique blend of surfactants—compounds that reduce the surface tension of the goop clinging to surfaces. The surfactants in Red Juice break this surface tension and allow the dirt to float away.

The surfactants in Red Juice are derived from sea kelp, among other things. What is *not* in it is also important: it lacks the surfactant in many janitorial and retail general-purpose cleaners—something called Butyl Cellosolve (2-butoxyethanol or closely related compounds). Butyl Cellosolve was formulated 25 to 30 years ago. According to California law,[1] it is listed as a "chemical contaminant" and described as being easily absorbed through the skin. (Maybe that's why it irritates the lungs so quickly.) It injures the kidneys and liver, irritates the eyes and mucous membranes,[2] and is listed as "very toxic" by an established textbook on toxicology.[3]

Needless to say, we were delighted to find a cleaner that didn't contain a drop of Butyl Cellosolve. Red Juice has the USDA's highest approval classification (A-1), meaning that it can be used on equipment in which food is made and on all surfaces of meat and dairy plants. It is nontoxic, odorless, and quickly and easily biodegradable (in 4 to 7 days).

Red Juice cannot be registered as a disinfectant because it lacks "killability" (thank goodness): it does not kill living cells on contact. But it cleans so well that bacteria and fungi have just about nothing to feed on, so the microbe count after cleaning a surface is close to zero.

We like Red Juice so well that we diluted it and colored it blue to make Blue Juice, which is the way we use and sell it. Its weaker concentration is all that's needed for cleaning glass surfaces. Both the red and blue dyes are included in the USDA A-1 approval. If you'd like to order our Red or Blue Juice, see page 191.

Alternatives

A solution of white vinegar and water is recommended by some sources. (Start with ¼ cup white vinegar to 1 quart water.) Or try 4 tablespoons baking soda per quart of water.[4] Don't expect either of these alternatives to have much cleaning strength.

Chlorine Bleach

We recommend the use of only a tablespoon or so of laundry-strength chlorine bleach—and then only if there is a mildew problem in the bathroom. We also dribble it on other mildewed surfaces—we don't spray it in a fine mist. This amount of bleach thus applied, especially rinsed with sufficient cold water afterward, does not appear to pose a significant environmental threat. Although chlorine bleach can be an individual health hazard in large enough amounts, we found no data on the environmental effects of the release of household-level amounts of chlorine bleach. Chlorine bleach in household quantities rapidly breaks down to a variety of common salts when it gets past the sink's P trap and enters the common drainage system.

Clorox states that its bleach is safe for septic systems—at least in standard household amounts. Its chlorine bleach is registered with the EPA as a disinfectant and contains no phosphates.

If you are concerned about use of chlorine bleach in your home, consider using a more dilute solution. Clorox recommends a dilution of 1 part Clorox to 21.33 parts water (that's ¾ cup per gallon of water) for anti-mildew operations, which is much more dilute than what we use (one to four). If you are concerned, you could experiment to find the most dilute solution that is still effective against the particular species of mildew in your home.

Alternatives

If you prefer not to use chlorine bleach at all, the alternative most commonly mentioned in the literature is a solution of borax and water. For example, Greenpeace[5] recommends a dilution of ½ cup borax per gallon of water. Powdered borax is available in the laundry section of larger grocery stores. We found no data showing that borax is effective against mildew or safe for the environment either, but it is less irritating than chlorine bleach for personal use.

Mildew can actually thrive in a mildly acidic environment, so vinegar and other acidic solutions that have been suggested for mildew treatments are not sensible alternatives.

Clorox recommends that no other cleaner—including baking soda—be mixed with bleach except a small amount of detergent as an option.

Comet

The active ingredient of environmental consequence in Comet and many other powdered scouring cleansers is a small percentage of chlorine bleach. We recommend its use, but in much smaller amounts than most housecleaners are inclined to use.

If you want to reduce your exposure to bleaching cleansers, consider using chemically resistant gloves, be careful about ventilation, and rinse the surfaces with cold water. (Steam from hot water may carry the chlorine into the air.)

Alternative

If you want to use an unbleached scouring powder, try Bon Ami, which is a relatively mild abrasive powder without chlorine or any other type of bleach. Some sources recommend baking soda, but it's an alkaline substance that can damage vulnerable surfaces itself if left unrinsed. And it often dissolves as it is being scrubbed on surfaces just when you need it most.

Paper Towels

As you've read, 100 percent cotton napkins and cloth diapers are our first and second choices for spray-and-wipe operations. Our third alternative is paper towels.

The quality of consumer paper towels varies enormously, and we believe it is a false economy to use the bargain brands because you'll end up using more of them to do the job. We prefer the Bounty Microwave brand. No inks or dyes are used in their manufacture, as is the case with most other pure-white paper towels. In addition, only materials approved by the Food and Drug Administration are voluntarily used in their manufacture. (Paper towels are normally not regulated by the FDA.) According to their manufacturer, there are no dioxins in this paper product—measured to one part per trillion.

Few, if any, unbleached paper towels are available in grocery stores. Many environmental workers are concerned about the effects on our water supplies of dioxins produced by the bleaching of wood pulp. Bleaches are added to pulp to purify it and make it more absorbent, among other reasons. The bleaches are not the problem. But they can lead to the production of dioxins when they react with certain ingredients of natural wood pulp. It is the dioxins that are the problem. The good news is that the paper industry is developing new technologies, including ones that use oxygenated bleaches so dioxins aren't produced. Other operating and processing innovations have been or will be introduced so the risk of dioxin release should be greatly diminished or eliminated for this industry.

Alternatives
Clean with reusable cotton cleaning cloths.

Ammonia

Anyone who has used ammonia cannot long remain unaware that ammonia is a powerful irritant to the lungs, eyes, and skin. But from an environmental point of view, sources differ considerably on its use.

Some recommend it as an alternative to traditional strong cleaners like oven cleaners. Others say to minimize its use because it is an irritant. We could find no data on the environmental impact of household levels of ammonia. But it is a compound that occurs spontaneously in nature—especially that part of nature near cat boxes. And it is an eminently biodegradable product.

Used in the amounts we recommend for washing floors, it is hard to conceive of it as an environmental threat. But be careful about pouring it down the toilet! If you installed a dispensing chlorine product in the toilet tank, keep the ammonia entirely away from the toilet.

Alternatives

There aren't many comparable alternatives for floor cleaning. You might try a solution of ¼ to 1 cup of white vinegar per gallon of water for most types of floor. But test in an inconspicuous spot first, because some types of floor (e.g., marble) do not like to be cleaned with any type of acid—even a mild one like vinegar.

Oven Cleaner

We use the standard formula of Easy Off oven cleaner, but we ask that it be applied the night before without heating the oven, so we don't have to deal with any fumes. And we use long, heavy industrial gloves when wiping out the oven. By the way, please ignore well-intentioned but misguided suggestions in some environmental publications to apply oven cleaner when the oven is already warm after cooking (to save energy). If you've misjudged and sprayed an already hot oven, you could be exposed to very harmful fumes. Better to spray a cool oven, close the door, and then heat it—per instructions.

The active ingredient in many oven cleaners is a serious compound: sodium hydroxide (lye). We found no data on environmental harm caused by household concentrations of oven cleaner. However, most formulas are notoriously caustic, which means they can burn and destroy skin tissue. Easy Off is now sold in at least two noncaustic varieties that contain no lye, and Arm & Hammer also has a noncaustic variety. All of these formulas are sold in manual pump-spray containers, not aerosols. They require a heated oven and overnight application. One or more of the formulas are so mild that their label instructions say you don't even have to wear gloves, but it's such a messy job that gloves would still seem to be a good idea.

Alternatives

The alternative to oven cleaners most often recommended in publications[6] is a bowl of ammonia left overnight in the oven. Add ¼ to ½ cup ammonia in a shallow glass or porcelain (not metal) bowl, plus about the same amount of warm water. Place the bowl in the oven and close the door. The idea is that fumes from the evaporating ammonia soften the crud in the oven overnight. Make sure the kitchen window is wide open before you lower the oven door the next day, because you will be greeted by obnoxious ammonia fumes. Wet the surfaces with Red Juice or the equivalent before scrubbing, and follow the procedures described in Chapter 7 for cleaning an oven.

The best way to reduce the amount of oven cleaner used is prevention, of course. Positioning a large baking sheet beneath the item being baked is one of those splendid ideas that one always remembers after the fact. Putting a piece of aluminum foil on top of that same tray is the other great idea.

Tile Juice

Most liquid tile cleaners that are designed to remove soap scum and mineral deposits are formulated around some type of acid—typically phosphoric acid.

Phosphoric acid does biodegrade, but unfortunately it biodegrades to form phosphate salts. Phosphates indirectly kill fish and other aquatic life by promoting the growth of algae that use up the available oxygen in rivers and lakes.

Because of the phosphate problem, we have switched our formula for Tile Juice to a neutral tile-cleaning solution that contains no phosphates, is biodegradable, and is nonacidic.

Alternatives

An alternative is white vinegar—another acid, but this time it's 5 percent acetic acid (the weakest type of acid). If you want to try vinegar, mix ½ cup or so of white vinegar per gallon of water, apply and scrub like Tile Juice, and rinse afterward. The white pad might be better than the tile brush for a thin liquid like vinegar. Some environmentalists suggest a paste of baking soda as an alternative (see Note 4). And there are new environmentally oriented product lines[7] that use citric acid (plus other ingredients) instead of phosphoric acid in their tile cleaners. Similar products are listed in *The Green Consumer*.[8]

Yet another choice is to stick to traditional powdered cleanser—chlorinated or otherwise—scrubbed with the tile brush. It's considerably more difficult to manage than a liquid cleaner, but it is not an acidic product.

Prevention is one of the wisest environmental steps you can take in terms of tile cleaning. The buildup from hard water is one reason that tile is difficult to clean, so consider installing a water softener. Or wipe down the shower walls and doors afterward with a quick swipe with a squeegee left in the shower for that purpose. If soap builds up quickly on your shower walls, changing soaps may help. For example, switch from a hard bar soap to a liquid soap or one that is milled with oils instead of fats.

Furniture Polish

The "lemon" Old English polish we have used for ten years has never caused us breathing difficulties. We find that the manual spray-pump formula works better than the aerosol (they are different formulas). It's fortunate that the product that works better is also safer environmentally.

There is concern that furniture polishes can cause harm to children who inhale their vapors. Polishes that have a high concentration of low-viscosity (thin) oils can, if inhaled, coat the lungs and seriously interfere with a child's ability to breathe. This formula of Old English has relatively little oil (less than 10 percent), and the oil is of high viscosity. If it is inhaled, the probability of causing respiratory distress is relatively slight. If drunk, it is usually nontoxic. But needless to say, it and all other furniture polish must be kept away from little ones, and any significant accidental exposure warrants medical advice.

Alternatives

If you prefer to use an oil instead of wax, you might consider plain walnut oil. After all, it came from wood to begin with. (We are absolutely amazed that some environmental publications recommend using mineral oil on wood furniture.) Many aficionados of fine wood furniture eschew oil in favor of paste wax. You can reduce airborne exposure to the oils in furniture polish by using a paste wax. Kiwi Bois and Goddard's are two excellent brands.

Water

One of the major issues in terms of environmental impact of household cleaning is the conservation and protection of the drinking supply. In a few years we'll probably look back in wonder that we used to flush our toilets and water our lawns with drinking water. But for now, our goals are more modest: to use as little water as reasonably possible and not to damage the available sources.

We believe that our *SPEED CLEANING* methods minimize the use of water in several ways: by not using sponges, which require frequent rinsing; by avoiding the use of scouring powder on areas that are difficult to rinse; by training you not to rinse or wipe until the proper time (Rule 5); by training you to work from top to bottom, which eliminates needless rewashing and rerinsing (Rule 3); and by using a cotton scrub mop (the Sh-Mop) that requires far less water to clean floors.

Further Reading

Environmentally safe cleaning is obviously a complex issue; much more can be learned. If you are interested in reading further, please see one or more of the references at the end of this chapter. One of the most complete presentations of the environmental perspective to date is the *Guide to Hazardous Products Around the Home* by the Household Hazardous Waste Project.

Whatever your choices about cleaning products, remember that THE METHOD IS MORE IMPORTANT THAN THE PRODUCTS. We can assure you that the Speed Cleaning method we've described here works well with a whole range of products whose ultimate selection is up to you.

NOTES

1. *California Code of Regulations*, Title 8, *General Industry Safety Orders*, Sec. 5155.
2. Nick H. Proctor, James P. Hughes, and Michael L. Fischman, *Chemical Hazards of the Workplace*, 2nd ed. (Philadelphia: J. B. Lippincott, 1988).

3. Robert E. Gosselin, Roger P. Smith, Harold C. Hodge, and Jeanette E. Braddock, *Clinical Toxicology of Commercial Products*, 5th ed. (Baltimore: Williams and Wilkins, 1984).
4. Household Hazardous Waste Project, *Guide to Hazardous Products Around the Home*, 2nd ed. (Southwest Missouri State University, 1989. 901 South National, Box 108, Springfield, Missouri 65804. $9.95. 178 pp. Shipping/handling included. Missouri residents add $0.61 sales tax.)
5. Greenpeace Action, *Everyone's Guide to Toxics in the Home.* (1436 U Street, N.W., Suite 201-A, Washington, DC 20009. 4 pp. Or request from your local chapter of Greenpeace.)
6. Center for Science in the Public Interest, *The Household Pollutants Guide*, ed., Albert J. Fritsch (Garden City, NY: Anchor Books, 1978).
7. Ecolo-Clean, Inc. (800) 373-5606.
8. John Elkington, Julia Hailes, and Joel Makower, *The Green Consumer* (New York: Penguin, 1990).

APPENDIX A:
Spanish Summary

THE CLEAN TEAM

Resumen de nuestro método de Limpieza Rápida*

Nuestro grupo, conocido en inglés como "The Clean Team," presta servicios de aseo doméstico en San Francisco aproximadamente 15,000 veces al año. Hemos perfeccionado un método de aseo que requiere más o menos la mitad del esfuerzo que la mayoría de las personas usa. Este capítulo describe nuestro método en forma resumida para aquellas personas que limpian sus hogares cada semana o dos veces al mes.

Nuestro método de limpieza es muy eficiente, es decir, elimina el gasto innecesario de esfuerzo, movimiento y tiempo. En cuanto mayor sea la eficiencia con que usted trabaje, menor cansancio sentirá. Y si se le hace difícil encontrar el tiempo necesario para completar sus labores,

nuestro método le ayudará a terminar mucho más rápido, aplicando más ingenio y menos esfuerzo.

Las reglas de nuestro método

1. No vuelva sobre sus pasos. Avance alrededor de cada pieza una sola vez, llevando consigo sus materiales.
2. Trabaje con utensilios apropiados, especialmente un buen delantal que le permita transportar sus materiales a medida que avanza en la pieza. Esto es esencial.

*Versión en español de: *In Other Words . . . Inc.*, Berkeley, California, EE.UU.

3. Trabaje siempre de arriba abajo.

4. Si algo no está sucio, no lo limpie. Por ejemplo, las superficies verticales generalmente están más limpias que las horizontales. Y ocurre con frecuencia que es necesario limpiar sólo las manchas hechas con los dedos y no toda la superficie.

5. No enjuague ni seque una superficie antes de que esté limpia. Si se equivoca, tendrá que volver a comenzar. Mientras la superficie esté todavía mojada con la solución de limpieza, verifique que esté limpia tocándola con el cepillo que está usando o con la punta de los dedos.

6. No siga trabajando después de verificar que está limpia. Si presta atención, se dará cuenta cuando ya lo está y podrá seguir adelante.

7. Si ve que su trabajo no le da un buen resultado, cambie de utensilio o use un agente limpiador más potente.

8. Mantenga sus utensilios en excelentes condiciones. De lo contrario, perderá tiempo o dañará superficies.

9. Con la repetición se simplifican los movimientos. Guarde siempre sus utensilios en el mismo sitio o bolsillo de su delantal.

10. Preste atención a lo que está haciendo.

11. Use ambas manos. Por ejemplo, sostenga un espejo con una mano mientras lo limpia con la otra.

12. Si se presenta la oportunidad, trabaje en equipo.

Utensilios y productos

Hemos descubierto que no es necesario usar una gran cantidad de productos especializados. Las cosas que usamos son las siguientes:

Un buen delantal: Nuestro delantal facilita las tareas de limpieza más que todos los otros productos juntos. Está diseñado con siete bolsillos, tres de los cuales son para los primeros tres utensilios descritos a continuación. En el cuarto bolsillo se guardan temporalmente basuritas, para evitar idas y venidas durante la limpieza.

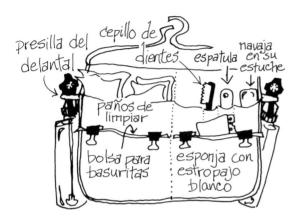

Un "cepillo de dientes." Este es un cepillo parecido a un cepillo de dientes normal, pero con cerdas más fuertes. Con él puede limpiar esquinas y ranuras que el paño de limpieza no alcanza.

Navaja en su estuche de seguridad. Para no hacer rayas, úsela solamente en superficies húmedas.

Espátula. Con una hoja de 1½″.

Bandeja. Le permite llevar los materiales de un lado a otro.

"Jugo" Rojo ("Red Juice"—en una botella rociadora). Nuestro líquido de limpieza profesional para trabajos pesados. Es parecido a los productos "409" y "Fantastik." Uselo para tareas de rociado y limpieza, excepto en espejos y ventanas.

"Jugo" Azul ("Blue Juice"—en una botella rociadora). Nuestro líquido de limpieza profesional para trabajos livianos. Es parecido a "Windex." Uselo para limpiar vidrios.

Blanqueador (en una botella rociadora). Uselo en el cuarto de baño solamente para eliminar el moho. Dilúyalo con por lo menos quatro partes de agua por cada parte de blanqueador. Uselo con mucho cuidado: el blanqueador puede dañar casi cualquier superficie. NO LO MEZCLE NUNCA con amoníaco u otro agente limpiador, ni lo use siquiera en combinación con estos productos.

"Jugo" para Azulejos ("Tile Juice"). Nuestro líquido de limpieza profesional para eliminar la acumulación de residuos de jabón y minerales del agua en los azulejos. Es parecido a "Lime-a-Way."

Plumero. Debe estar fabricado con las plumas suaves del avestruz.

Paños para limpiar. Los mejores son los de 100% de algodón. Nosotros usamos servilletas hechas de paño. A falta de servilletas, lo mejor son pañales de algodón; y por último, toallas de papel marca "Bounty Microwave."

Líquido para lustrar muebles (con botella rociadora). Nosotros utilizamos "Old English" en la botella rociadora.

Paño para lustrar muebles. Use el tipo sin sustancias químicas si es posible. No use este paño para ninguna otra tarea de limpieza.

Agente limpiador en polvo. Nosotros usamos "Comet."

Botella de plástico de una pinta. Use esta botella para ayudarse a enjuagar la tina de baño y la ducha si es necesario.

Escobilla. Elija una con cerdas de plástico.

Cordón eléctrico de extensión de 50 pies de largo, con su carrete. Para la aspiradora.

Cepillo para el inodoro. Elija uno con cerdas de plástico (que no tenga alambre trenzado).

Cepillo para azulejos. Es un cepillo grande con cerdas largas de plástico.

Combinación esponja-estropajo blanco. Consiste en una esponja con un estropajo blanco en uno de sus lados. Se usa cuando un paño no da resultado.

Trapeador. Nosotros utilizamos un maravilloso trapeador de algodón perfeccionado, el llamado "Sh-Mop." (Vea la ilustración en la pág. #15.)

Líquido para limpiar pisos. Una solución de amoníaco es barata y muy eficaz.

Estropajo de virutas de acero. Compre el más fino (número 000).

Usted puede pedir que le mandemos directamente por correo cualesquiera de estos utensilios de limpieza. Para obtener gratis nuestro catálogo, escríbanos a la siguiente dirección:

The Clean Team
2264 Market Street
San Francisco, CA 94114

O llámenos al teléfono (415) 621-8444.

La cocina

El punto de partida. Apoye el trapeador en la pared, al lado de la puerta de entrada. Coloque la bandeja sobre el mostrador, inmediatamente a la derecha del fregadero. En la bandeja tendrá: El agente limpiador en polvo, los Jugos Rojo y Azul, la combinación esponja-estropajo blanco, el plumero, la escobilla y aproximadamente una docena de paños de limpiar lavados y doblados. En los bolsillos del delantal tendrá la espátula, el cepillo de dientes, la navaja en su estuche de seguridad y dos bolsas de plástico para forrar los bolsillos.

Vestimenta de trabajo. Vístase con pantalones que tengan bolsillos traseros. Póngase el delantal, amarrándose las tiras con firmeza alrededor de la cintura. Cuelgue las botellas de Jugo Rojo y Azul de las presillas del delantal. (Vea la ilustración en la pág. #20.)

Si decide colocar la botella de Jugo Azul del lado izquierdo, póngala siempre de ese lado para que la pueda alcanzar sin detenerse a mirar. Es posible que las tapas de las botellas rociadoras se aflojen; por lo tanto, debe desarrollar el hábito de apretarlas cuando las recoge por primera vez al comenzar a trabajar. Coloque el plumero en uno de los bolsillos traseros y la escobilla en el otro. Tome de la bandeja entre 8 y 10 paños de limpiar y métalos en el bolsillo del delantal. (Vea la ilustración en la pág. #20.)

Preparativos. Saque el bote de basura de la cocina y déjelo al lado de la puerta. Si hay alfombras pequeñas, sáquelas y déjelas extendidas sobre el piso al lado de la puerta. (Vacíe el bote de basura y pase la aspiradora a las alfombras más tarde.)

Manchas de dedos en alacenas y mostradores. Empezando del lado derecho del fregadero, trabaje avanzando siempre hacia la derecha, sin retroceder, y llevando consigo todos sus utensilios y limpiando de arriba abajo en cada parte. Sobre el mostrador por lo general hay alacenas y, como están arriba, empiece con ellas. En la mayoría

de los casos, lo único que tendrá que limpiar son las manchas hechas con los dedos alrededor de los tiradores de las puertas. Las manchas deben limpiarse con Jugo Rojo; por lo tanto, saque la botella de la presilla del delantal y rocíe el área ligeramente. Con una mano, vuelva a colgar la botella de la presilla del delantal mientras emplea la otra mano para secar el área con uno de los paños de limpiar. Recuerde la Regla 4: Si solamente necesita limpiar una o dos manchas en una puerta de alacena que por lo demás está limpia, limítese a rociar las manchas y pasarles el paño. Le tomará unos 5 segundos. No se dé el trabajo adicional de rociar toda la puerta.

Luego, rocíe y limpie el mostrador de atrás para adelante. Hágalo generalmente con la botella de Jugo Rojo en una mano y el paño de limpiar en la otra. Cuando encuentra un artefacto sobre el mostrador, como por ejemplo la tostadora, muévala hacia usted, limpie el área donde se encontraba, limpie la tostadora, vuelva a ponerla en su lugar, y limpie luego el área del mostrador delante de ella.

Después de limpiar la parte del mostrador delante de usted, siga con las puertas o gabinetes debajo de él. Examine los tiradores para ver si tienen manchas. Si las tienen, quítelas con el cepillo de dientes y el Jugo Rojo y luego seque el área con el paño. Cuando el paño se ensucia demasiado o se empapa, métalo en el bolsillo del delantal forrado con la bolsa de plástico o en la bandeja.

Acostúmbrese a colgar siempre las botellas rociadoras de las presillas del delantal, sin ponerlas sobre el mostrador. Al principio esto puede parecer una molestia, pero al hacerlo comprobará que su trabajo es más sencillo y placentero cuando tiene siempre a su alcance lo que necesita. Esto se convertirá pronto en hábito.

Problemas con el mostrador. Cuando encuentra un punto difícil de limpiar sobre el mostrador, acuda a los utensilios de mayor potencia. La mayoría del tiempo el Jugo Rojo y el paño serán suficientes. Si no obtiene resultados con el paño, use el estropajo blanco o la espátula (Regla 7). A veces encontrará que aun con el estropajo blanco es muy difícil sacar restos secos de comida (p. ej.

gotas de mezcla para panqueques endurecidas hasta convertirse en hormigón). Cuando encuentra este tipo de problema, no intente siquiera limpiarlo con el paño. Usando la espátula, podrá aflojarlo en cuestión de segundos. Tenga cuidado de no rayar la superficie: remoje primero la superficie con Jugo Rojo, y mantenga el ángulo de la espátula bien bajo. (Vea la ilustración en la pág. #27.)

Cuadros con vidrio, ventanas de vidrio y espejos. Rocíelos ligera y uniformemente con Jugo Azul. Mientras el vidrio esté todavía mojado, use la navaja sobre cualquier mancha seca de pintura u otro tipo de sucio difícil de quitar. (Pero no use la navaja en superficies de plástico.) Frote el vidrio con un paño muy seco hasta secarlo. Si no lo seca completamente, quedarán manchas. Y si el paño no está muy seco, tendrá que trabajar demasiado porque tomará más tiempo secar el vidrio.

Telarañas. Mire la pared hasta el cielo raso cada vez que da otro paso hacia la derecha. Si ve una telaraña, use el plumero que lleva en uno de los bolsillos traseros. Si no puede alcanzarla, inserte el mango del plumero en uno de los tubos de extensión de la aspiradora, añadiendo otro si es necesario. (Vea la ilustración en la pág. #12.)

Estantes. Para limpiar estantes, mueva primero todas las cosas hacia la derecha. Limpie el lado izquierdo, mueva todas las cosas hacia la izquierda y limpie el lado derecho. Luego, vuelva a poner todo en su sitio. Si hay demasiadas cosas sobre el estante, ponga algunas sobre el mostrador o sobre el piso para dejar espacio.

El exterior del refrigerador. Limpie primero la parte de arriba. Es posible que sólo tenga que desempolvarla con el plumero. Limpie las manchas hechas con los dedos sobre el exterior de la puerta. Abra la puerta y limpie la junta de la puerta y cualquier derrame pequeño que pueda limpiar con facilidad sin mover cosas dentro del refrigerador.

La parte superior de la cocina de gas o eléctrica.

Limpie primero el área encima de la cocina. Ponga los filtros en el lavaplatos si necesitan lavarse.

Cocinas de gas. Primero, ponga las parrillas de la izquierda sobre las parrillas de la derecha. Rocíe el lado izquierdo con Jugo Rojo, use el estropajo blanco y seque el área con un paño. Vuelva a colocar las parrillas de la izquierda y ponga las de la derecha sobre el mostrador junto a la cocina, del lado derecho. Limpie ahora el lado derecho de la misma manera y vuelva a colocar las parrillas de la derecha en su sitio.

Si no puede limpiar la parte superior de la cocina con el estropajo blanco, saque el limpiador en polvo de la bandeja. Riegue una cantidad *pequeña* de polvo sobre el área problemática y frótela ligeramente con el estropajo blanco. Use el estropajo de virutas de acero (000) *sólo* si el estropajo blanco no le da resultado. Pero tenga mucho cuidado con el estropajo de virutas de acero, porque puede rayar muchas superficies y las rayas pueden ser difíciles de ver. Haga primero la prueba en un punto poco visible.

Cocinas eléctricas. Normalmente se puede limpiar alrededor de los anillos de cromo o aluminio rociándolos con Jugo Rojo y usando el cepillo de dientes. Use el estropajo blanco para limpiar el metal propiamente dicho. Luego, seque el área con el paño. Como de costumbre, trabaje de atrás para adelante y de izquierda a derecha.

La parte delantera de la cocina. Puede limpiar los botones de control de los quemadores rociándolos con Jugo Rojo y usando el cepillo de dientes. Abra la puerta del horno para limpiar el interior de la ventana del horno con Jugo Rojo y la navaja.

El fregadero. Complete su vuelta alrededor de la cocina limpiando el fregadero. Limpie el área encima del borde de atrás y alrededor del grifo con Jugo Rojo y un paño. (*No use* limpiador en polvo.) Cada vez que limpia, use el cepillo de dientes alrededor del grifo y las manijas, y en el borde donde el fregadero se une al mostrador.

Remoje el interior del fregadero. Riegue limpiador en polvo ligeramente en el fondo y los lados del fregadero y use el estropajo blanco en esta área. Luego, enjuague completamente. Use el polvo únicamente *por debajo* del borde porque es difícil de enjuagar en otras áreas del fregadero.

Ponga el Jugo Rojo y el Jugo Azul junto con el plumero en la bandeja y saque la bandeja de la cocina, dejándola al lado de la puerta. Tome la solución para limpiar pisos (p. ej. el amoníaco) y póngala en un bolsillo del delantal.

El piso. Primero, barra el piso o pase la aspiradora. Lleve el trapeador al fregadero. Llene un balde o el fregadero hasta ⅓ con agua tibia y agréguele de ¼ a ½ taza de amoníaco (o su producto preferido para limpiar pisos). El trapeador que nosotros usamos tiene una cubierta removible fabricada de tela de toalla. Quite la cubierta, moje el trapeador en el balde o en el fregadero, tuérzalo hasta dejarlo bastante seco, vuelva a ponerle la cubierta y comience a trapear el piso. Enjuague la cubierta cuando sea necesario. Cuando termine de trapear el piso, vacíe el agua, enjuague la cubierta del trapeador y el interior del fregadero, y seque el área alrededor del grifo con un paño. ¡Felicitaciones! Ya terminó de limpiar la cocina.

El cuarto de baño

Deje la bandeja con sus utensilios en el piso del lado derecho de la tina de baño. Ponga en el delantal los mismos utensilios que utilizó en la cocina. Limpie el baño avanzando de izquierda a derecha, como hizo en la cocina. Pero haga dos vueltas alrededor del cuarto de baño en vez de una: la primera para limpiar las áreas mojadas (ducha, tina, lavabo e inodoro); y la segunda para limpiar el resto del cuarto.

Las paredes de la ducha. Ponga en el piso los objetos que encuentre al borde de la tina. Remoje las paredes con agua. Tome de la bandeja el Jugo para Azulejos y rocíe las paredes, empe-

zando con la pared opuesta al tubo de drenaje. Use el cepillo para azulejos solamente para distribuir el Jugo de manera uniforme sobre las superficies. No las restriegue todavía. Cubra con el líquido todas las áreas que requieran limpieza (inclusive las puertas de la ducha). Ponga el Jugo para Azulejos nuevamente en la bandeja. Ahora, restriegue las paredes de la ducha, empezando por la que roció primero con el Jugo. El cepillo para azulejos penetra bien los espacios entre los azulejos. Si es posible, quédese fuera de la tina para hacer este trabajo. El fondo de la tina se pone muy resbaladizo durante la limpieza.

Las puertas corredizas de la ducha y sus guías. Como el cepillo para azulejos no funciona tan bien sobre el vidrio como sobre los azulejos, limpie el interior de la puerta de la ducha con el estropajo blanco. Si la ducha tiene cortina, no trate de limpiarla a mano: póngala en la máquina lavadora con una toalla si es del tipo lavable.

Por lo general es posible limpiar las guías de las puertas corredizas con el cepillo de dientes y el Jugo Rojo. Si esto no le da resultados, use la espátula cubierta con un paño, o doble el estropajo blanco en dos. *No enjuague nada todavía.*

La tina. Saque el limpiador en polvo de la bandeja y espolvoree un poco uniformemente en el fondo y en los lados de la tina. No lo aplique a las paredes de la ducha ni a los artefactos de plomería, sino solamente en la tina misma.

Usando el cepillo para azulejos, comience a limpiar la tina desde el extremo opuesto al tubo de drenaje. Use el cepillo de dientes en los bordes donde la tina se une a los azulejos, eliminando así la mayor parte del moho que puede estar acumulándose allí. Si queda algo de moho, puede usar el blanqueador más tarde.

Enjuague de la ducha y tina. Una vez que quede limpio todo el interior de la ducha y tina, ponga el cepillo para azulejos *sin enjuagar* en el lavabo y déjelo allí por el momento. Ahora puede comenzar el enjuague.

Abra la llave de la regadera. Si tiene suerte, estará conectada a una manguera, con lo cual se facilitará mucho el enjuague. Enjuague las paredes y puertas completamente antes de enjuagar la tina. Esta vez, comience con la pared que esté *más cerca* del tubo de drenaje, enjuagando de arriba hacia abajo. Si hay áreas que no puede alcanzar con la regadera, use la botella de plástico que tiene en su bandeja. Luego, enjuague la tina, pero esta vez empiece por el extremo *opuesto* al tubo de drenaje.

El interior del lavabo. El cepillo para azulejos se encuentra todavía en el lavabo y está todavía lleno del limpiador en polvo utilizado en la tina. Uselo sin añadir más polvo y limpie solamente el interior del lavabo, no los bordes ni el grifo.

Cuando termine de limpiar el lavabo, enjuague el cepillo, póngalo en la bandeja y enjuague el lavabo. No se preocupe, el borde del lavabo y el grifo se lavarán después. Tome ahora el cepillo del inodoro y el agente limpiador en polvo.

El interior del inodoro. Remoje el cepillo para limpiar el inodoro sumergiéndolo en la taza. Espolvoree un poco de agente limpiador sobre el cepillo y alrededor del interior de la taza. Comience por la parte de arriba y avance en forma circular hasta llegar al fondo de la taza.

La segunda vuelta

A medida que limpiaba la taza, también enjuagaba el limpiador en polvo del cepillo. Sacuda el cepillo para sacarle el exceso de agua y guárdelo en la bandeja. Tire de la cadena para vaciar el inodoro.

Usted ha completado ahora la primera vuelta, o sea la limpieza con agua. La siguiente vuelta es para la limpieza algo más seca. Ponga el plumero en su bolsillo trasero, saque de la bandeja entre 8 y 10 paños de limpiar y métalos en el delantal. Limpie las cosas a medida que las va encontrando: por ejemplo, los espejos, manchas de dedos, telarañas, toalleros, el botiquín, el borde del lavabo, las bandejas de vidrio para maquillaje y el exterior de las puertas de la ducha.

Cuando llega al inodoro, límpielo de la siguiente manera. Rocíe y limpie el tanque. Levante la tapa y el asiento. Rocíe la superficie inferior del asiento y bájelo. Rocíe la superficie superior del asiento. Rocíe la superficie inferior de la tapa y bájela también. Rocíe la superficie superior de la tapa y detrás de ella hasta alcanzar los goznes. Use el cepillo de dientes según sea necesario en los goznes y en los protectores de caucho del asiento y de la tapa. Enjuague en el orden inverso. Por último, rocíe y limpie el resto del inodoro y también el piso alrededor de la base. Continúe ahora su avance alrededor del cuarto de baño.

El piso. Si el piso está cubierto con alfombra, pase la aspiradora cuando va a usarla en el resto de la casa. De lo contrario, tome varios paños para limpiar el piso. Arrodíllese en la esquina opuesta a la salida. Comience a rociar el piso con el Jugo Rojo y a pasarle el paño mientras retrocede hasta salir del cuarto. Dele vuelta frecuentemente al paño para no dejar marcas.

El blanqueador. Después de terminar con el piso, si queda todavía algo de moho en el área de la ducha o de la tina, éste es el momento de rociarlo con la solución blanqueadora. Saque de la bandeja la botella del blanqueador para rociar y ajuste la boquilla para que eche "chorritos" en vez de "rocío." De esta manera, reduce a un mínimo la cantidad de blanqueador que pueda inhalar. Aplique el blanqueador directamente sobre las áreas mohosas. Nosotros suspendemos la respiración al aplicar el blanqueador y salimos del cuarto de baño para respirar aire fresco si toma demasiado tiempo aplicarlo. Seque de inmediato con el paño cualquier gota de blanqueador que caiga sobre superficies metálicas. Para ayudar a evitar fugas accidentales, cubra la boquilla de la botella de blanqueador con un paño viejo cuando termina de usarlo. (Una gota que caiga sobre una alfombra dejará un mancha blanca permanente.) Guarde la botella del blanqueador en la bandeja de utensilios y saque la bandeja del cuarto de baño, dejándola al lado de la puerta. Si ha utilizado blanqueador para eliminar moho, vuelva dentro de 5 minutos para enjuagar el blanqueador. ¡Felicitaciones! Acaba de completar otra tarea.

Desempolvar y pasar la aspiradora

Esta parte de la limpieza se hace más rápido porque es más seca y generalmente no hay que rociar y secar tanto. De nuevo, comience en un sitio y avance dentro de cada pieza sin dar marcha atrás, siguiendo las reglas ya explicadas.

Para desempolvar, es especialmente importante trabajar de arriba abajo. Usted sentirá el impulso natural de limpiar primero lo que encuentre por delante, o lo que le parezca interesante o sea fácil de alcanzar. En vez de ello, forme el hábito de mirar *hacia arriba*, examinando *primero* las molduras, la parte superior de los cuadros, las luces y las telarañas, de manera que no se cree más trabajo ensuciando superficies que ya limpió.

Utensilios de trabajo. Para esta tarea no necesitará el limpiador en polvo, el Jugo para Azulejos, el estropajo blanco o el blanqueador; saque por lo tanto todo eso de la bandeja. Sustitúyalos por el líquido y el paño para lustrar muebles, junto con cualquier otro producto (p. ej., líquido o pasta para lustrar plata) que pueda necesitar para la casa específica que está limpiando. Puede sacar también la bolsa de plástico que usó para forrar el bolsillo donde llevaba el estropajo blanco. Use ahora el mismo bolsillo (sin la bolsa de plástico) para transportar el líquido y el paño para lustrar muebles. Muchas personas prefieren comenzar por la sala. Ponga la bandeja de utensilios en el piso de esa pieza, justo al lado de la puerta, y comience a limpiar avanzando de izquierda a derecha y de arriba abajo.

El uso del plumero. Al finalizar el movimiento de limpieza con el plumero (p. ej., al extremo del marco de un cuadro), detenga el plumero por completo. No deje que el movimiento del plumero continúe en el aire más allá del cuadro, porque esto esparcirá polvo que se depositará sobre los muebles que usted acaba de limpiar. Para sacar el polvo que se ha acumulado en el plumero, dé unos golpecitos con el plumero sobre su tobillo, cerca del piso. Esto tiene como propósito depositar el polvo en el piso, de donde lo sacará con la aspiradora.

Complete la limpieza de cada área a medida que pasa por ella. Antes de avanzar, haga todo lo que tiene que hacer en esa área: desempolvar, lustrar, frotar, cepillar, rociar y secar, y arreglar las cosas en su sitio. Cambie de utensilios de limpieza cada vez que sea necesario: por ejemplo, si está desempolvando tranquilamente con el plumero y encuentra manchas de fruta en conserva sobre el televisor, ¡zas!, guarde el plumero en el bolsillo trasero con una mano mientras saca la botella de Jugo Rojo con la otra. Rocíe la mancha con esa mano mientras saca con la primera el paño de limpiar. Frote la mancha con esa mano mientras usa la otra para devolver la botella a su sitio en la presilla del delantal. Luego, guarde el paño en el bolsillo del delantal mientras alcanza el plumero con la mano libre. Ahora puede seguir adelante.

El uso de la aspiradora. Puede pasar la aspiradora con mucho más facilidad si hace algunos preparativos mientras desempolva. Por ejemplo:

1. Use el plumero (sobre un piso de madera) o la escobilla (en una alfombra) alrededor de las patas de las mesas, sillas, camas, etc. Esto saca el polvo que está justamente al lado de la pata, polvo que la aspiradora siempre deja. Lo mismo ocurre con el borde de la alfombra junto a las paredes y en la escalera, donde la aspiradora deja sin limpiar más o menos la última pulgada.

2. Si sobre el sofá hay solamente algunas migajas o pelos de gato, use la escobilla.

3. Al pasar la aspiradora, use un cordón eléctrico de extensión de 50 piés de largo, para que no tenga que conectarla y desconectarla más de una vez. Para evitar que se desconecte la aspiradora mientras la usa, haga un pequeño nudo para unir el cordón eléctrico de extensión con el cordón de la aspiradora. (Vea la ilustración en la pág. #90.)

¿Y eso es todo? ¡Eso es todo! Como toda destreza recién adquirida, la Limpieza Rápida requiere aprendizaje, práctica, repaso y perfeccionamiento. Pero vale la pena. Usted se convertirá en un experto o una experta en el arte de limpiar casas. Y esto le facilitará su trabajo, eliminando estrés y aumentando su productividad. Esta será su recompensa.

Buena suerte y . . . ¡Manos a la obra!

APPENDIX B:
How to Order Tools, Equipment, and Supplies

It makes little sense to us to write about a cleaning method if we don't offer some way of enabling you to find the products we mentioned.

Because we use cleaning products daily and test new ones continuously, we have developed very definite opinions about them. We know what works and won't tolerate anything that doesn't. Some of the products have a higher initial cost, but they last two or three times longer than the cheaper alternatives. Others have replaceable parts that save money in the long run. And others cost more but just plain work better. For example, even if those cheap chicken feather dusters were free, we still wouldn't use them because they don't work. We much prefer to pay a fair price for ostrich-down feather dusters that work and that save time week after week. And if something new comes along that works better, we change products. We aren't committed to any brand name or manufacturer—only to excellence.

One way to save time in your own housecleaning is not to have to endure all the tests and trials of products that we do. But even if you know what products you want to use, it still takes time to purchase them—especially if they're not carried at the local grocery or hardware store, which is true of many of the professional products we use. Our catalog can save you time on both accounts, because you can make your choices without leaving your home.

The only products we offer are the same ones we actually use in the field all day long. There's only one heavy-duty liquid cleaner, for example, because that's the best one we've found so far— and we're still looking after 12 years.

If you would like a free copy of our catalog, please write us at:

The Clean Team
206B N. Main Street
Jackson, CA 95642

If you're in a hurry, call us at 800-238-2996 and we'll mail you one the same day.

Or visit our Website @
www.the cleanteam.com.